# MEAT & POULTRY

**Text by Judith Ferguson**
**Photography by Peter Barry**
**Designed by Philip Clucas**
**Produced by Ted Smart and David Gibbon**

CLB 1678
© 1986 Illustrations and text: Colour Library Books Ltd.,
    Guildford, Surrey, England.
Text filmsetting by Focus Photoset Ltd., London, England.
Printed and bound in Barcelona, Spain.
All rights reserved.
ISBN 0 86283 478 3 (Softback)
ISBN 0 86283 477 5 (Hardback)

# *Microwave*
# MEAT & POULTRY

# CONTENTS

When you cook in a microwave oven you get far more for your meat money. Microwave roasting means less shrinkage and, contrary to popular belief, meat *will* brown. Leave a thin layer of fat on the roast/joint, or rub butter into a chicken or turkey and the high heat of the microwave oven will turn the fat golden brown. Alternatively, there are many marinades, bastes and coatings to give appetizing color to meat, poultry and game.

Because liquids evaporate much more slowly in a microwave oven, there will be more meat juices left to make good sauces and gravies. If you want, use a browning dish to brown the flour for gravies. Red wine, soy sauce, gravy browning and spices also give good color to brown sauces.

In general, stews and braises should be cooked on MEDIUM, regardless of what variety of meat is used. The highest setting in a microwave oven will toughen the cuts of meat used in stews and braises. When cooking small cuts of meat such as chops or steaks in a sauce, a medium setting is also recommended for a tender result. Stir-frying and pan-frying are both possible with a browning dish and the highest setting. Offal/variety meats cook very quickly, so a high setting suits them as well.

When roasting poultry and game birds, cover the legs and wings with foil to prevent them from drying out. Uncover for a portion of the cooking time and the whole bird will be evenly cooked. Depending on your oven, you may find that all roast meats need to be covered with foil on both ends for part of their cooking time. This is especially important for roasts/joints that are uneven in thickness.

Microwave roasts must be left to stand after cooking just like any roast meat. The standing time helps to finish off the cooking, so microwaved roast meat, poultry and game are usually covered for 5-15 minutes before carving.

Special microwave meat thermometers take the guesswork out of roasting, but times will vary from oven to oven. The following chart will serve as a quick reference, but is meant only as a guideline.

| Time and Setting per 450g/1lb | | |
|---|---|---|
| | **HIGH** | **MEDIUM** |
| **Beef**<br>Rare<br>Medium<br>Well done | 6-7 minutes<br>7-8 minutes<br>8-9 minutes | 11-13 minutes<br>13-15 minutes<br>15-17 minutes |
| **Chicken** (whole) | 6-8 minutes | 9-11 minutes |
| **Duck** (whole) | 6-8 minutes | 9-11 minutes |
| **Leg of Lamb** | 8-10 minutes | 11-13 minutes |
| **Pork** | 9-11 minutes | 13-15 minutes |
| **Veal** | 8-9 minutes | 11-12 minutes |
| **Steaks** (7.5cm/1½″ thick)<br>Rare<br>Medium rare<br>Medium<br>Well done | 9 minutes<br>10 minutes<br>12 minutes<br>14 minutes | |

There is also a method of roasting, Hazelnut Lamb is an example, which cuts down on the cooking time and depends on a longer standing time to finish cooking to the desired doneness. Also, meats and poultry can be roasted for part of their cooking time on HIGH and part on MEDIUM.

All the recipes were tested in both a conventional 700 watt microwave oven and a Combination microwave-convection oven with a maximum setting of 600 watts. The Combination oven does a superb job of roasting. It is nearly as fast as the conventional microwave oven, yet browns and crisps like a regular convection oven. These new ovens have a variety of settings, so it is best carefully to follow the instruction booklet that each manufacturer provides. Either way, the time saving is impressive, and the result delicious when a microwave oven is used on meat, poultry and game.

# LAMB DISHES

## Lamb Shanks with Leeks and Rosemary

**PREPARATION TIME:** 15 minutes

**MICROWAVE COOKING TIME:** 45 minutes

**SERVES:** 4 people

*30ml/2 tbsps vegetable oil*
*900g-1kg/2-2¼ lbs lamb shanks*
*1 clove garlic, roughly chopped*
*2 sprigs fresh rosemary*
*280ml/½ pint/1 cup red wine*
*280ml/½ pint/1 cup beef stock*
*15g/1 tbsp butter*
*15g/1 tbsp flour*
*2-4 leeks, washed and thinly sliced*
*Salt and pepper*

Heat the oil in a browning dish for 5 minutes on HIGH. Put in the lamb shanks and cook for 5 minutes on HIGH. Turn the lamb over and cook for further 5 minutes on HIGH. Add the garlic, rosemary, salt and pepper, wine and stock. Cover and cook on MEDIUM for 25 minutes. Melt the butter in a small bowl for 30 seconds on HIGH. Stir in the flour. Pour on the cooking juices from the lamb and stir well. Pour the sauce over the lamb and scatter over the sliced leeks. Cook a further 5 minutes on HIGH, until the leeks soften and the sauce has thickened. Remove the rosemary before serving.

## Spiced Lamb Chops with Peaches

**PREPARATION TIME:** 15 minutes

**MICROWAVE COOKING TIME:** 20 minutes

**SERVES:** 4 people

*4 lamb chops, fat slightly trimmed*
*30g/1oz/2 tbsps butter or margarine*
*15ml/1 tbsp ground allspice*
*15ml/1 tbsp ground ginger*
*15ml/1 tbsp brown sugar*
*Salt and pepper*
*225g/8oz sliced peaches, juice reserved*
*45ml/3 tbsps soy sauce*
*45ml/3 tbsps brown sugar*
*30ml/2 tbsps cider vinegar*
*5ml/1 tsp cornstarch/cornflour*
*10ml/2 tsps water*

**This page: Spiced Lamb Chops with Peaches (top) and Lamb Shanks with Leeks and Rosemary (bottom). Facing page: Orange Glazed Lamb with Haricot Beans.**

Heat a browning dish for 5 minutes on HIGH. Drop in the butter and heat 30 seconds on HIGH. Mix 15ml/1 tbsp brown sugar with the spices, salt and pepper and rub into both sides of the chops. Fry the chops in the butter on HIGH for

2 minutes each side. Mix the peach juice with the soy sauce, remaining brown sugar, vinegar and additional salt and pepper. Pour over the chops and cover loosely. Lower the setting to MEDIUM and cook 10 minutes, turning the chops once and stirring the liquid frequently. Remove the chops and set aside to keep warm. Mix the cornstarch/cornflour with the water and stir into the hot liquid. Cook on HIGH for 1 minute, stirring frequently until the sauce is clear. Add the peaches to heat through for 30 seconds on HIGH and serve with the chops.

## Lamb in Sour Cream Dill Sauce

**PREPARATION TIME:** 15 minutes

**MICROWAVE COOKING TIME:** 31 minutes

**SERVES:** 4 people

900g/2lbs leg of lamb, cut into 2.5cm/ 1 inch cubes
1 onion, sliced
1 bay leaf
15ml/1 tbsp dried dill or dill seed
430ml/¾ pint/1½ cups light stock
140ml/4 fl oz/½ cup white wine
45g/1½ oz/3 tbsps butter or margarine
45g/1½ oz/3 tbsps flour
30g/2 tbsps chopped fresh dill or 15g/ 1 tbsp dried dill
140ml/¼ pint/½ cup sour cream
Salt and pepper

Make sure all the fat is trimmed from the lamb. Put the lamb cubes, onion, bay leaf, dried dill or dill seed, salt, pepper, stock and wine into a casserole. Cover and cook on MEDIUM for 25 minutes. Set aside to keep warm. Melt the butter 30 seconds on HIGH. Stir in the flour and strain on the stock from the lamb. Stir well and cook for 5 minutes on HIGH, stirring frequently, until thickened. Add the dill, adjust the seasoning and stir in the sour cream. Pour over the lamb and heat through 1 minute on HIGH, without boiling. Serve with rice or pasta.

## Orange Glazed Lamb with Haricot Beans

**PREPARATION TIME:** 15 minutes

**MICROWAVE COOKING TIME:** 24 minutes

**SERVES:** 4 people

2 racks/best-end necks of lamb

**GLAZE**
60g/2oz/¼ cup dark brown sugar
60ml/2 fl oz/¼ cup red wine
15ml/1 tbsp red wine vinegar
Juice and rind of 1 orange

**ACCOMPANIMENT**
450g/1lb canned haricot/navy beans or flageolets, drained
4 green/spring onions, chopped
60ml/2 fl oz/¼ cup dry white wine
Pinch thyme
Salt and pepper

Trim some of the fat from the lamb and score the remaining fat. Mix the glaze ingredients together and brush over the lamb. Put the lamb on a roasting rack. The bone ends may be covered with foil to protect them during the cooking. Cook on MEDIUM for 10 minutes. Raise the setting to HIGH and cook for 5 minutes, basting often during the whole of the cooking time. Leave to stand 5 minutes before carving. Cook for 20 minutes on the Combination setting of a microwave convection oven until the fat has browned. Mix the beans, wine, onions, thyme, salt and pepper together and cook 4 minutes on HIGH. Reheat any remaining glaze and pour over the lamb. Serve with the beans.

## Peppercorn Lamb

**PREPARATION TIME:** 13 minutes

**MICROWAVE COOKING TIME:** 21-22 minutes

**SERVES:** 4 people

675g/1½ lbs lamb fillet or meat from the leg cut into 5mm/¼ inch slices
60g/2oz/4 tbsps butter or margarine

2 shallots, finely chopped
1 clove garlic, finely minced
45g/1½ oz/3 tbsps flour
5ml/1 tsp ground allspice
280ml/½ pint/1 cup beef stock
15ml/1 tbsp canned green peppercorns, rinsed and drained
2 caps pimento cut into thin strips
5ml/1 tsp tomato paste/purée
60ml/2 fl oz/¼ cup heavy/double cream
Salt and pepper

Heat a browning dish for 5 minutes on HIGH. Melt the butter for 1 minute on HIGH and add the slices of lamb. Cook for 2 minutes on HIGH, in 2 or 3 batches. Remove the meat and set aside. Cook the shallots and flour to brown slightly. Add the garlic, allspice, stock and tomato paste/purée. Season with salt and pepper and cook 2-3 minutes on HIGH, until starting to thicken. Add the lamb, cover and cook 10 minutes on MEDIUM, or until the lamb is tender. Add the peppercorns, pimento and cream and cook for 2 minutes on HIGH. Serve with rice.

## Leg of Lamb with Aromatic Spices

**PREPARATION TIME:** 15 minutes

**MICROWAVE COOKING TIME:** 31 minutes, plus 5-15 minutes standing time

**SERVES:** 6-8 people

1.5kg/3lbs leg of lamb, fat completely trimmed off
140ml/¼ pint/½ cup stock

**MARINADE**
280ml/½ pint/1 cup plain yogurt
1 small piece fresh ginger root, grated
5ml/1 tsp crushed coriander seeds
1.25ml/¼ tsp cloves
5ml/1 tsp curry powder
5ml/1 tsp cumin
1.25ml/¼ tsp cardamom seeds, removed from the pods
1 clove garlic, minced
Salt and pepper

**Facing page: Lamb in Sour Cream Dill Sauce (top) and Peppercorn Lamb (bottom).**

**SAUCE**
*Remaining marinade and stock*
*15ml/1 tbsp chopped fresh coriander*
*140ml/¼ pint/½ cup plain yogurt*

Blend all the marinade ingredients together. In the lamb, make incisions with a sharp knife about 5cm/ 2 inches apart. Place the lamb in a shallow casserole. Push some of the marinade into each cut and spread the remaining marinade over the surface of the lamb. Cover and leave overnight in the refrigerator. Pour the stock into the casserole around the lamb. Cover the casserole loosely and cook on HIGH for 12 minutes, basting frequently. Turn the lamb over and cook a further 15 minutes, basting frequently. Leave the lamb to stand for 5 minutes in a covered dish if serving rare. For well-done or medium lamb leave it to stand for 15-20 minutes. Meanwhile heat the remaining marinade and stock for 3 minutes on MEDIUM. Stir in the yogurt and coriander leaves. Add more salt and pepper if necessary and heat through 1 minute on HIGH. Do not allow the sauce to boil. Serve with the carved lamb.

## Hazelnut Lamb

**PREPARATION TIME:** 15 minutes

**MICROWAVE COOKING TIME:**
25-30 minutes, plus
5-15 minutes standing time

**SERVES:** 6-8 people

*2kg/4½ lbs leg of lamb*
*1 clove garlic, finely minced*
*120g/4oz/1 cup dry breadcrumbs*
*120g/4oz/1 cup ground, roasted hazelnuts*
*30ml/2 tbsps chopped parsley*
*60g/2oz/¼ cup butter*
*Salt and pepper*

Trim the fat off the lamb. Mix together the remaining ingredients except the breadcrumbs. Spread the hazelnut paste over the surface of the lamb and press over the crumbs. Cook 25-30 minutes on MEDIUM. Increase the setting to HIGH for 2 minutes. Cook 40 minutes on a Combination setting of a microwave

convection oven. Leave the lamb to stand, loosely covered, 5 minutes before carving for rare. Leave 10-15 minutes if medium to well-done lamb is desired. Serve with minted new potatoes and peapods/mangetout.

## Moroccan Lamb

**PREPARATION TIME:** 20 minutes

**MICROWAVE COOKING TIME:**
35 minutes

**SERVES:** 4 people

*790g/1¾ lbs lamb fillet or meat from the leg cut in 2.5cm/1 inch cubes*
*1 clove garlic, minced*
*10ml/2 tsps ground cinnamon*
*1.25ml/¼ tsp ground cloves*
*1.25ml/¼ tsp ground cumin*
*10ml/2 tsps paprika*

**This page: Hazelnut Lamb. Facing page: Leg of Lamb with Aromatic Spices.**

*1 large red pepper*
*570ml/1 pint/2 cups light beef stock*
*340g/¾ lb okra, trimmed*
*120g/¼ lb/1 cup whole blanched almonds*
*60g/2oz/¼ cup currants*
*15ml/1 tbsp honey*
*15ml/1 tbsp lemon juice*
*Salt and pepper*

Combine the lamb, garlic, spices, red pepper, salt and pepper in a large casserole. Add the stock, cover the dish and cook on MEDIUM for 25 minutes. Add the okra, currants and almonds. Cook a further 5 minutes on MEDIUM. Remove the

setting of a microwave convection oven for 15 minutes or until potatoes are cooked and slightly browned. Three minutes before the end of cooking time, arrange the pepper rings overlapping on top of the potatoes. Garnish with fresh bay leaves to serve.

## Navarin of Lamb

**PREPARATION TIME:** 20 minutes

**MICROWAVE COOKING TIME:** 40 minutes

**SERVES:** 4 people

*4 lamb chops*
*30ml/2 tbsps oil*
*30g/2 tbsps flour/plain flour*
*2 cloves garlic, finely minced*
*15ml/1 tbsp tomato paste/purée*
*280ml/½ pint/1 cup white wine*
*570ml/1 pint/2 cups stock*
*2 sprigs fresh rosemary or 15ml/1 tbsp dried*
*1 sprig fresh thyme or 5ml/1 tsp dried*
*Salt and pepper*

**GARNISH**
*2 carrots, cut lengthwise in quarters*
*120g/4oz green/French beans, trimmed and cut in 5cm/2 inch pieces*
*8 small new potatoes, scrubbed but not peeled*
*2 sticks celery, cut in 5cm/2 inch strips*
*12 small mushrooms, left whole*
*4 small turnips, peeled*

Heat a browning dish 5 minutes on HIGH. Pour in the oil and put in the lamb chops. Cook 1 minute on HIGH. Turn the chops over and cook 2 minutes on HIGH on the other side. Remove the chops and stir in the flour, tomato purée/paste, wine, stock and garlic. Cook for 2 minutes on HIGH, stirring twice. Season with salt and pepper and return the chops to the dish or transfer the whole to a casserole. Cover and cook on MEDIUM for 15 minutes. Add the vegetables, except the beans and mushrooms, and cook 15 minutes further on MEDIUM. Add remaining vegetables 5 minutes before the end of cooking. Remove the herbs, if using fresh, and the bay leaf before serving.

meat and vegetables and almonds to a serving dish. Add the honey and lemon juice to the sauce and cook on HIGH for 5 minutes to reduce it slightly. Pour over the lamb and serve with rice.

## Lamb Hot-Pot

**PREPARATION TIME:** 15 minutes

**MICROWAVE COOKING TIME:** 30 minutes

**SERVES:** 4 people

*2 large onions, peeled and thinly sliced*
*30ml/2 tbsps oil*
*450g/1lb ground/minced lamb*
*30ml/2 tbsps chopped parsley*
*Pinch thyme*
*225g/8oz whole mushrooms*
*225g/8oz/1 cup canned tomatoes*
*30ml/2 tbsps Worcestershire sauce*
*3 potatoes, peeled and thinly sliced*
*1 red pepper, cut in rings*
*1 green pepper, cut in rings*
*Salt and pepper*

**This page: Navarin of Lamb. Facing page: Moroccan Lamb (top) and Lamb Hot-Pot (bottom).**

**GARNISH**
*Fresh bay leaves*

In a large casserole, heat the oil for 30 seconds on HIGH. Put in the onions and cover the casserole loosely. Cook 5 minutes on HIGH to soften the onions. Add the lamb and thyme and cook 10 minutes on MEDIUM, mashing the lamb with a fork to break it up while it cooks. Add the mushrooms, tomatoes, parsley, salt and pepper and Worcestershire sauce. Arrange the slices of potato neatly on top of the lamb mixture and sprinkle with more salt and pepper. Cover the casserole and cook on MEDIUM for 15 minutes or until the potatoes are tender. Cook on a Combination

# PORK AND HAM

## Glazed Ham and Spiced Peaches

**PREPARATION TIME:** 20 minutes

**MICROWAVE COOKING TIME:**
57 minutes, plus
5 minutes standing time

**SERVES:** 6-8 people

1.5kg/3lb ham/gammon, boneless and
　pre-cooked

**GLAZE**
30ml/2 tbsps Dijon mustard
120g/4oz/½ cup dark brown sugar
120g/4oz/1 cup dry breadcrumbs
Pinch powdered cloves
Pinch ginger

**PEACHES**
6 fresh peaches or 12 canned peach halves
120g/4oz/½ cup light brown sugar
5ml/1 tsp each ground cinnamon, cloves
　and allspice
140ml/¼ pint/½ cup water or canned
　peach juice
30ml/2 tbsps cider vinegar
12 walnut halves

If using fresh peaches, put them into
a large bowl and cover with boiling
water. Heat on HIGH for 3 minutes
or until the water boils. Peel the
peaches, cut in half and remove the
stones. Mix the remaining ingredients
for the peaches together and heat
2 minutes on HIGH, stirring
frequently until the sugar dissolves.
Add the peaches and cook 2 minutes
on MEDIUM. Remove the peaches
and cook the syrup a further
5 minutes on HIGH. Pour the syrup
over the peaches and set them aside.
Cover the ham with plastic wrap/
cling film, or put into a roasting bag.

**This page: Pork à l'Orange. Facing
page: Glazed Ham and Spiced
Peaches.**

Cook on MEDIUM for 15 minutes
per lb or ½ kg. Pour the glaze over
during the last 10 minutes of cooking.
Put a walnut half in the hollow of
each peach. Let the ham stand
5 minutes before slicing. Serve either
hot or cold with the peaches.

## Pork à l'Orange

**PREPARATION TIME:** 15 minutes

**MICROWAVE COOKING TIME:**
24-25 minutes

**SERVES:** 4 people

30g/2 tbsps butter or margarine
675g/1½ lbs pork tenderloin/fillet cut in
　1.25cm/½ inch slices
3 carrots, cut in 1.25cm/½ inch diagonal
　slices
3 small or 2 large leeks, washed and
　trimmed and cut in 1.25cm/½ inch
　diagonal slices
60g/2oz/¼ cup dried currants

1 clove garlic, finely minced
1 large onion, sliced
1 large green pepper, sliced
120g/4oz mushrooms, sliced
15ml/1 tbsp tomato paste/purée
30ml/2 tbsps molasses/treacle
225g/8oz canned tomatoes
1 bay leaf
Pinch Cayenne pepper
Salt and pepper

Melt the butter in a casserole for
30 seconds on HIGH and put in the
pork pieces, garlic, onions and
mushrooms. Cook 5 minutes on
MEDIUM. Add the remaining
ingredients and cook a further
5 minutes on MEDIUM, loosely
covered. If the pork is not tender
after 10 minutes, cook an additional
3 minutes on MEDIUM. Remove the
bay leaf before serving.

## Ginger Apricot Stuffed Pork

**PREPARATION TIME:** 15 minutes

**MICROWAVE COOKING TIME:**
33-34 minutes, plus
5 minutes standing time

**SERVES:** 6-8 people

1.5kg/3lbs loin of pork, boned
570ml/1 pint/2 cups light stock
1 bay leaf
1 carrot, sliced

**STUFFING**
120g/4oz/¾lb dried apricots
30ml/2 tbsps green ginger wine
30ml/2 tbsps lemon juice
60ml/2 fl oz/¼ cup water
1 spring/green onion, finely chopped
Salt and pepper

**SAUCE**
280ml/½ pint/1 cup strained reserved
    stock from the pork
Apricot soaking liquid
30g/1oz/2 tbsps butter or margarine
30g/1oz/2 tbsps flour
Dash soy sauce

Mix the stuffing ingredients, except
the onion, together in a bowl. Cover
well and cook 1 minute on HIGH,
then leave to stand to soften the

1.25ml/¼ tsp ground ginger
1 bay leaf
280ml/1½ pints/1 cup orange juice
60ml/2 fl oz/¼ cup orange liqueur
10ml/2 tsps cornstarch/cornflour
Salt and pepper

Heat a browning dish 5 minutes on
HIGH. Drop in the butter and add
the pork slices. Cook 2 minutes each
side on HIGH. Cook the meat in 2
or 3 batches. Add the leeks, carrots,
bay leaf, ginger, salt and pepper. Pour
over the orange juice and cover the
dish loosely. Cook 15 minutes on
MEDIUM or until the pork and
vegetables are tender. Add the
currants during the last 3 minutes of
cooking. Remove the pork and
vegetables and keep them warm.
Mix the liqueur and cornstarch/
cornflour together and stir into the
sauce. Cook, uncovered, 2 to 3

**This page: Ginger Apricot Stuffed
Pork. Facing page: Pork Creole
(top) and Sausages, Apples and
Cheese (bottom).**

minutes on HIGH, stirring frequently
until the sauce thickens and looks
clear. Return the meat and vegetables
to the sauce and stir carefully.
Serve with rice.

## Pork Creole

**PREPARATION TIME:** 15 minutes

**MICROWAVE COOKING TIME:**
13 minutes

**SERVES:** 4 people

15ml/1 tbsp butter
750g/1½ lbs lean pork shoulder or
    tenderloin/fillet cut into strips

apricots. Trim most of the fat from the pork. Turn the meat over and sprinkle the surface with pepper. Drain the apricots and reserve the juice. Spread the apricots evenly over the pork and sprinkle on the onion. Roll up the pork starting on the thickest side. Tie at even intervals with string. Place in a deep casserole with the bay leaf, stock and carrot. Cover well and cook 30 minutes on MEDIUM or until the pork is tender and no longer pink. Strain the stock and reserve it. Cover the pork and leave to stand 5 minutes before slicing. Melt the butter in a deep bowl for 30 seconds on HIGH. Stir in the flour and 280ml/½ pint/1 cup stock and the reserved apricot juice. Cook 2 to 3 minutes on HIGH to thicken. Add salt and pepper to taste and serve with the pork.

## Speedy Ham Casserole

**PREPARATION TIME:** 10 minutes

**MICROWAVE COOKING TIME:** 6 minutes

**SERVES:** 4 people

225g/8oz cooked ham, cut in 1.25cm/ ½ inch strips
1 can concentrated cream of mushroom soup
1 can water chestnuts, drained and sliced
2 sticks celery, finely chopped
225g/8oz frozen, sliced green/French beans
30ml/1 fl oz/2 tbsps dry sherry
280ml/½ pint/1 cup light/single cream
Pinch thyme
Salt and pepper

**TOPPING**
1 can French-fried onions
or
60g/2oz/¼ cup seasoned breadcrumbs mixed with 5ml/1 tsp paprika

Mix all the ingredients, except the topping ingredients, together in a serving casserole. Cook 5 minutes on HIGH, stirring occasionally, or until the beans have cooked. Sprinkle on the topping and cook a further 1 minute on HIGH.

## Sweet and Sour Ham

**PREPARATION TIME:** 20 minutes

**MICROWAVE COOKING TIME:** 2-3 minutes

**SERVES:** 4 people

450g/1lb cooked ham, cut into 1.25cm/ ½ inch cubes

**SAUCE**
60g/2oz/¼ cup brown sugar
60ml/2 fl oz/¼ cup rice vinegar
30ml/2 tbsps tomato ketchup
30ml/2 tbsps soy sauce
225g/8oz/1 can pineapple chunks/ pieces, drained and juice reserved
30g/1oz/2 tbsps cornstarch/cornflour
1 green pepper, sliced
2 green/spring onions, sliced diagonally
60g/2oz/½ cup blanched, whole almonds
3 tomatoes, quartered
Salt and pepper

Combine the sugar, vinegar, ketchup, soy sauce, cornstarch/cornflour and reserved pineapple juice and chunks. Add pepper, almonds, salt, pepper and ham. Cook 2-3 minutes on HIGH until the sauce clears and thickens. Add the tomatoes and green/spring onions and heat 30 seconds on HIGH. Serve with rice or crisp noodles.

## Sausages, Apples and Cheese

**PREPARATION TIME:** 15 minutes

**MICROWAVE COOKING TIME:** 10-12 minutes

**SERVES:** 4 people

1 ring smoked sausage
4 medium cooking apples, cored and thinly sliced
30ml/2 tbsp brown sugar
30ml/2 tbsp flour
1 shallot, finely chopped
15ml/1 tbsp chopped sage
120g/4oz/1 cup shredded Cheddar cheese
Pinch salt and pepper

Toss the apples, brown sugar, flour,

sage and onion together. Slice the sausage in 1.25cm/½ inch diagonal slices and arrange on top of the apples. Cover loosely and cook on HIGH 5 to 7 minutes or until the apples are tender. Sprinkle over the cheese and cook 5 minutes on Medium to melt. Serve immediately.

## Ham Loaf with Mustard Chive Sauce

**PREPARATION TIME:** 15 minutes

**MICROWAVE COOKING TIME:** 27-28 minutes, plus 5 minutes standing time

**SERVES:** 4 people

340g/12oz/¾ lb ground/minced, cooked ham
340g/12oz/¾ lb ground/minced pork
60g/2oz/½ cup dry breadcrumbs
140ml/¼ pint/½ cup milk
2 shallots, finely chopped
1 clove garlic, crushed
Salt and pepper

**SAUCE**
45g/1½ oz/3 tbsps butter or margarine
45g/1½ oz/3 tbsps flour/plain flour
30ml/2 tbsps Dijon mustard
280ml/½ pint/1 cup milk
140ml/¼ pint/½ cup light stock
30ml/2 tbsps chopped chives
Salt and pepper

Combine all the ingredients for the ham loaf and press into a glass loaf dish. Cook on HIGH for 5 minutes. Reduce setting to MEDIUM, cover with plastic wrap/cling film and cook 20-25 minutes, or until firm. Turn the dish after 10 minutes. Leave in the dish for 5 minutes before turning out to slice. Melt the butter for the sauce 30 seconds on HIGH. Stir in the flour and remaining ingredients, except for the chives. Cook 2-3 minutes on HIGH, stirring often until thick. Add the chives and serve with the ham loaf.

**Facing page: Speedy Ham Casserole (top) and Sweet and Sour Ham (bottom).**

## Cranberry-Orange Ham Slices

**PREPARATION TIME:** 10 minutes

**MICROWAVE COOKING TIME:** 7-9 minutes

**SERVES:** 4 people

*4 ham steaks*
*15g/1 tbsp butter or margarine*

**SAUCE**
*Juice and rind of 1 orange*
*225g/8oz whole cranberry sauce*
*60ml/2 fl oz/¼ cup red wine*
*5ml/1 tsp cornstarch/cornflour*
*1 bay leaf*
*Pinch salt and pepper*

**GARNISH**
*1 orange, sliced*

Heat a browning dish 5 minutes on HIGH. Put in the butter and brown the ham 2 minutes on the first side and 1 minute on the other. Combine sauce ingredients in a small, deep bowl. Cook 1-2 minutes on HIGH, until the cornstarch/cornflour clears. Remove the bay leaf and pour over the ham to serve. Garnish with the orange slices.

## Polynesian Ham Steaks

**PREPARATION TIME:** 20 minutes

**MICROWAVE COOKING TIME:** 9-10 minutes

**SERVES:** 4 people

*4 ham steaks*
*15ml/1 tbsp oil*
*1 small fresh pineapple, sliced*
*1 papaya, sliced*
*2 bananas, peeled and sliced*
*1 fresh coconut, grated*
*280ml/½ pint/1 cup orange juice*
*Juice and grated rind of 1 lime*
*10ml/2 tsps cornstarch/cornflour*
*30ml/2 tbsps brown sugar*

Heat a browning dish 5 minutes on HIGH. Add the oil to the dish and lay in the ham steaks. Cook 2 minutes on the first side and 1 minute on the other. Set the ham

aside. Combine the orange juice, lime juice and rind, cornstarch/cornflour and sugar in a large bowl. Cook 1-2 minutes on HIGH, stirring frequently until thickened. Add the fruit and coconut and heat through 1 minute on HIGH. Pour over the ham steaks to serve.

## Swedish Meatballs

**PREPARATION TIME:** 15 minutes

**MICROWAVE COOKING TIME:** 13-15 minutes

**SERVES:** 4 people

**This page: Cranberry-Orange Ham Slices (top) and Polynesian Ham Steaks (bottom). Facing page: Ham Loaf with Mustard Chive Sauce.**

**MEATBALLS**
*225g/8oz ground/minced pork*
*225g/8oz ground/minced beef*
*225g/8oz ground/minced veal*
*2 shallots, finely chopped*
*60g/2oz/¼ cup dry breadcrumbs*
*Pinch ground cloves, nutmeg and allspice*
*60ml/2 fl oz/¼ cup milk*
*1 egg, beaten*
*Salt and pepper*

**SAUCE**
*30g/1oz/2 tbsps flour/plain flour*
*280ml/½ pint/1 cup milk*
*140ml/¼ pint/½ cup light/single cream*
*10ml/2 tsps fresh dill or 5ml/1 tsp dried dill*
*15ml/1 tsp lemon juice*
*5ml/1 tsp grated lemon rind*
*Salt and pepper*

Combine all the meatball ingredients in a large bowl and mix very well. Shape into 2.5cm/1 inch balls and arrange in a large baking dish. Cook, uncovered, for 10 to 12 minutes on HIGH, or until firm and no longer pink. Rearrange the meatballs twice during cooking, bringing the ones from the edges of the dish to the middle. When the meatballs are cooked remove them to a serving dish to keep warm. Stir in the flour and add the milk, cream, dill and salt and pepper. Cook, stirring frequently, 3 to 5 minutes on HIGH. Add the lemon juice and rind and pour over the meatballs to serve.

## Pork with Prunes and Apples

**PREPARATION TIME:** 15 minutes and 1 hour soaking time for prunes

**MICROWAVE COOKING TIME:** 26 minutes

**SERVES:** 4 people

*4 pork chops*
*120g/4oz/½ cup prunes, stones removed*
*580ml/1 pint/2 cups tea*
*2 apples, peeled and sliced*
*5ml/1 tsp lemon juice*
*Pinch mace*
*Pinch thyme*
*30g/1oz/2 tbsps butter*
*30g/1oz/2 tbsps flour/plain flour*
*140ml/¼ pint/½ cup heavy/double cream*

**GARNISH**
*Parsley sprigs*

Boil 580ml/1 pint/2 cups water in a covered bowl for 8 minutes on HIGH. Put in 2 tea bags and the prunes. Leave to soak 1 hour. Heat a browning dish 5 minutes on HIGH.

Melt the butter and brown the pork for 2 minutes on each side. Remove the chops and set aside. Add the flour to the dish and stir in well. Strain 280ml/½ pint/1 cup of the prune soaking liquid into the dish and add the lemon juice, mace, thyme, salt and pepper. Add the pork and cover the dish loosely. Cook 10 minutes on MEDIUM. Add the apples and prunes during the last 4 minutes of cooking. Stir in the cream and heat 1 minute on HIGH. Serve garnished with parsley sprigs.

## Italian Pork Rolls

**PREPARATION TIME:** 20 minutes

**MICROWAVE COOKING TIME:** 24 minutes

**SERVES:** 4 people

*4 pork escalopes or pork steaks*
*30g/1oz/2 tbsps vegetable oil*

**FILLING**
*60g/2oz/¼ cup ricotta cheese*
*60g/2oz salami, roughly chopped*
*120g/4oz/1 cup fresh breadcrumbs*
*120g/4oz/1 cup pimento stuffed olives, roughly chopped*
*60g/2oz/½ cup pistachio nuts*
*2 shallots, finely chopped*
*15ml/1 tbsp chopped basil*
*15ml/1 tbsp chopped parsley*
*Pinch oregano*
*Salt and pepper*
*1 egg, beaten*

**SALPICON**
*225g/8oz tomatoes, peeled, seeded and quartered*
*225g/8oz mushrooms, sliced*
*1 green pepper, cut in thin strips*
*1 onion, thinly sliced*
*60ml/2 fl oz/¼ cup dry white wine or vermouth*
*15ml/1 tbsp tomato paste/purée*
*Salt and pepper*

Flatten the pork pieces with a meat mallet or rolling pin until very thin. Mix the filling ingredients together and spread evenly over the meat. Roll up, tucking in the sides, and fasten with a wooden pick/cocktail stick. Heat a browning dish for 5 minutes on HIGH. Add the oil and

place in the pork rolls in a circle. Cover loosely and cook on MEDIUM for 10 minutes. Rearrange the rolls twice to cook evenly. Cook a further 3 minutes on MEDIUM if the pork is still pink. Remove to a serving dish to keep warm. Cook the onion and the mushrooms in the meat juices for 3 minutes on HIGH. Add the wine, purée/paste, peppers, allspice, salt and pepper. Cook further 2 minutes on HIGH. Add the tomatoes and cook 1 minute on MEDIUM to heat through. Remove the wooden picks from the pork and serve it with the salpicon.

## Pork with Plums and Port

**PREPARATION TIME:** 15 minutes

**MICROWAVE COOKING TIME:** 24-25 minutes

**SERVES:** 4 people

*675g/1½ lbs pork tenderloin/fillet cut in 1.5cm/½ inch slices*
*30g/1oz/2 tbsps butter or margarine*
*30g/1oz/2 tbsps flour*
*1 bay leaf*
*2 whole cloves*
*280ml/½ pint/1 cup stock*
*140ml/¼ pint/½ cup port*
*450g/1lb purple or red plums*
*Pinch sugar*
*5ml/1 tsp lemon juice*

**GARNISH**
*Chopped parsley*

Heat a browning dish 5 minutes on HIGH. Melt the butter and put in the pork slices. Cook 2 minutes each side. Cook in 2 to 3 batches. Remove the pork and stir in the flour. Cook 2 minutes on HIGH, stirring frequently to brown the flour lightly and evenly. Stir in the stock and port and add the cloves, bay leaf, salt and pepper. Replace the meat and cover the dish loosely. Cook 10 minutes on MEDIUM. Cut the plums in half and

**Facing page: Swedish Meatballs (top) and Pork with Prunes and Apples (bottom).**

remove the stones. Cut in quarters if the plums are large. Add to the meat and cook 5 minutes further on MEDIUM. Taste the sauce and add sugar and/or lemon juice to taste. Remove the bay leaf and cloves. Sprinkle on the chopped parsley before serving.

## Smoked Pork with Melon

**PREPARATION TIME:** 15 minutes

**MICROWAVE COOKING TIME:** 16 minutes

**SERVES:** 4 people

*1 small, ripe melon*
*90g/3oz peapods/mangetout*
*4 smoked pork chops, fat trimmed*
*15ml/1 tbsp butter or margarine*
*Grated rind and juice or 1 orange*
*Salt and pepper*
*Chopped parsley or coriander*

Scoop out the flesh of the melon in balls and set it aside. Spoon out any remaining flesh and blend with the orange juice, salt and pepper in a food processor. Add the orange rind. Trim the peapods/mangetout and cook 1 minute with 15ml/1 tbsp water in a covered bowl. Heat a

**This page: Italian Pork Rolls. Facing page: Pork with Plums and Port (top) and Smoked Pork with Melon (bottom).**

browning dish for 5 minutes on HIGH. Melt the butter and cook the chops 2 minutes each side on HIGH. Pour over the sauce and cook 5 minutes on MEDIUM. Add the reserved melon balls, peapods/mangetout and parsley or coriander. Heat 1 minute on HIGH before serving.

# BEEF, VEAL AND OFFAL

## Spinach and Ricotta Stuffed Veal

**PREPARATION TIME:** 25 minutes

**MICROWAVE COOKING TIME:** 34-35 minutes

**SERVES:** 6 people

900g-1.5kg/2-3lbs loin of veal, boned
   and trimmed
1 bay leaf
1 slice onion
280ml/½ pint/1 cup stock or water

**STUFFING**
450g/1lb fresh spinach, washed well
120g/4oz/½ cup ricotta cheese
1 egg, beaten
30g/2 tbsps pine nuts, roughly chopped
½ clove garlic, minced
5ml/1 tsp chopped basil
Grated nutmeg
Salt and pepper

**SAUCE**
Pan juices made up to 430ml/¾ pint/
   1½ cups with stock
30g/1oz/2 tbsps flour/plain flour
30g/1oz/2 tbsps butter or margarine
30ml/2 tbsps dry white wine
Salt and pepper

Cook the spinach with 15ml/1 tsp water for 2 minutes on HIGH, in a covered bowl. Drain well and chop roughly. Mix the remaining stuffing ingredients with the spinach and spread on one side of the veal. Roll up from the thicker end of the meat to the thin end. Tie at even intervals with string. Place in a casserole with 1 cup water or stock. Cover loosely and cook for 30 minutes on MEDIUM. Leave to stand 5 minutes before carving. Heat the butter 1 minute on HIGH and add the flour, stock, wine, salt and pepper. Stir to blend well and cook 2-3 minutes on HIGH, until thickened. Serve with the veal and a selection of vegetables.

**This page: Spinach and Ricotta Stuffed Veal. Facing page: Veal Involtini (top) and Veal Ragout (bottom).**

## Liver Lyonnaise with Orange

**PREPARATION TIME:** 20 minutes

**MICROWAVE COOKING TIME:** 13-18 minutes

**SERVES:** 4 people

450g/1lb liver, sliced
45g/1½ oz/3 tbsps flour
30g/1oz/2 tbsps butter or margarine
1 onion, sliced
Rind and juice of 1 orange
140ml/¼ pint/½ cup stock
Pinch thyme
Salt and pepper

**GARNISH**
Orange slices
Chopped parsley

Heat a browning dish 5 minutes on HIGH. Melt the butter in the dish for 1 minute on HIGH. Dredge the liver in the flour and add to the butter in the dish. Cook the liver for 1 minute on HIGH. Turn over and cook 1 minute further on HIGH. Remove from the dish. Cook the onions 1 minute on HIGH. Peel 1 orange and cut the peel into very thin strips. Squeeze the juice and add to the liver along with the remaining ingredients. Cook 10-15 minutes on MEDIUM, until the liver is tender. Turn the slices over frequently during cooking. Serve garnished with the orange slices and chopped parsley.

## Veal Involtini

**PREPARATION TIME:** 20 minutes

**MICROWAVE COOKING TIME:** 21-22 minutes

**SERVES:** 4 people

8 veal escalopes/cutlets
8 slices Parma ham
8 slices cheese
10ml/2 tbsps chopped sage
Salt and pepper
30ml/2 tbsps oil

**SAUCE**
1 400g/14oz can plum tomatoes
1 clove garlic, crushed
1 small onion, finely chopped
30ml/2 tbsps tomato purée
Pinch oregano
Pinch basil
Pinch sugar
1 bay leaf
Salt and pepper

Flatten the veal escalopes. Place on the ham and cheese and sprinkle on the sage, salt and pepper. Roll up, folding in the ends, and secure with wooden picks/cocktail sticks. Heat a browning dish 5 minutes on HIGH. Pour in the oil and heat 1 minute on HIGH. Add the veal rolls and cook 2 minutes, turning several times. Combine all the sauce ingredients in a deep bowl. Cook 3-4 minutes on HIGH. Remove bay leaf and blend in a food processor until smooth. Pour over the veal and cook, covered, on MEDIUM for 10 minutes. Serve with spinach.

## Veal Ragout

**PREPARATION TIME:** 20 minutes

**MICROWAVE COOKING TIME:** 37-41 minutes, plus 5 minutes standing time

**SERVES:** 4 people

450g-900g/1½-2lbs veal shoulder or leg cut in 2.5cm/1 inch cubes
2 onions, sliced
225g/8oz mushrooms, quartered
60g/2oz/¼ cup butter or margarine
60g/2oz/¼ cup flour/plain flour
10ml/2 tsps thyme
1 bay leaf
1 clove garlic, minced
570ml/1 pint/2 cups beef stock
30ml/2 tbsps tomato paste/purée
Salt and pepper

**ACCOMPANIMENT**
225g/8oz/3 cups pasta
120g/4oz/1 cup grated cheese

Heat a browning dish 5 minutes on HIGH. Melt the butter 1 minute on HIGH. Brown the meat in 2 batches

**Facing page: Liver Lyonnaise with Orange.**

5ml/1 tsp coarsely crushed black
 peppercorns
10ml/2 tsps mustard seeds
2 crushed bay leaves
10ml/2 tsps dill
5ml/1 tsp crushed allspice berries
430ml/¾ pint/1½ cups water
6 carrots, peeled and quartered lengthwise
2 small rutabaga/swedes, peeled and cut
 into wedges
6-8 small potatoes, peeled and left whole
1 large head of white cabbage, cut into
 wedges

Put the corned/salt beef, water, herbs
and spices into a large, deep
casserole. Cover tightly and cook on
HIGH for 8 minutes, or until the
water boils. Reduce the setting to
MEDIUM and cook 30 minutes,
covered. Turn over the meat and add
the carrots, potatoes and rutabaga/
swedes. Re-cover the dish and cook a
further 30-40 minutes on MEDIUM.
Add the cabbage 15 minutes before
the end of cooking. Leave to stand
for 10 minutes before slicing the meat
across the grain. Serve with the
vegetables and some of the cooking
liquid.

## Veal Parmesan with Courgettes/Zucchini

**PREPARATION TIME:** 20 minutes

**MICROWAVE COOKING TIME:**
17-22 minutes

**SERVES:** 4 people

4 veal escalopes/cutlets
4 courgettes/zucchini

**COATING**
30g/1oz/2 tbsps seasoned breadcrumbs
45g/1½ oz/3 tbsps grated Parmesan
 cheese
1 egg, beaten
Salt and pepper

on HIGH for 3 minutes per batch.
Cook the onions and mushrooms for
2 minutes on HIGH. Remove the
meat and vegetables, and stir in the
flour. Cook the flour for 3 minutes to
brown slightly. Add the remaining
ingredients and return the meat and
the vegetables to the dish, or transfer
to a casserole, cover and cook on
MEDIUM 15 minutes. Put the pasta
in water and partially cover with
plastic wrap/cling film. Cook
6-10 minutes on HIGH, stirring
occasionally. Leave to stand 5
minutes and drain and rinse in hot
water. Remove the bay leaf from the
ragout. Arrange the pasta in a serving

dish and spoon the ragout into the
middle. Sprinkle on grated cheese
and heat 1 minute on HIGH to melt
the cheese before serving.

## New England Boiled Dinner

**PREPARATION TIME:** 20 minutes

**MICROWAVE COOKING TIME:**
1 hour 8 minutes to 1 hour 18 minutes

**SERVES:** 6-8 people

900g-1.5kg/2-3lbs corned/salt beef
 brisket

**This page: New England Boiled
Dinner. Facing page: Veal
Parmesan with Courgettes/
Zucchini.**

## SAUCE

1 400g/14oz can plum tomatoes
1 clove garlic, crushed
1 small onion, finely chopped
30ml/2 tbsps tomato purée/paste
Pinch oregano
Pinch basil
Pinch sugar
Pinch grated nutmeg
1 bay leaf
Salt and pepper

## TOPPING

120g/4oz/1 cup mozzarella cheese
30g/2oz/¼ cup grated Parmesan cheese

Slice the zucchini/courgettes and cook 2 minutes on HIGH, with enough water to cover in a deep bowl. Mix the crumbs, Parmesan cheese, salt and pepper for the coating. Dip the veal in the egg and then in the breadcrumb coating. Put the veal into a shallow dish, cover loosely and cook 8-10 minutes. Do not turn the veal over, but rearrange once during cooking. Combine all the sauce ingredients in a deep bowl. Cook 3-4 minutes on HIGH. Arrange the courgette/zucchini slices in a serving dish, place the veal on top of the courgettes/zucchini and pour over the tomato sauce. Top with the mozzarella and Parmesan cheeses and cook 4-6 minutes on HIGH or Combination setting on a microwave convection oven. Serve immediately.

# Beef Enchiladas

**PREPARATION TIME:** 20 minutes

**MICROWAVE COOKING TIME:**
12-14 minutes

**SERVES:** 4 people

225g/8oz package tortillas

## SAUCE

1 onion, finely chopped
45ml/3 tbsps tomato purée/paste
1.2kg/1lb 10oz can tomatoes
1-2 small chili peppers, seeded and finely chopped
5ml/1 tsp ground coriander
1 bay leaf
Salt and pepper

## FILLING

30ml/2 tbsps oil
225g/8oz minced/ground beef
1 clove garlic, finely minced
10ml/2 tsps ground cumin
1 green pepper, roughly chopped
12 black olives, stoned and chopped
Salt and pepper

## GARNISH

1 avocado, sliced
120g/4oz/1 cup grated Cheddar or Monterey Jack cheese

If the tortillas are dry, brush them with water, cover in paper towels and heat 2 minutes on HIGH before rolling up. Combine all the sauce

**This page: Risotto Stuffed Peppers (top) and Beef Enchiladas (bottom). Facing page: Chicken Livers and Walnut Pasta (top) and Kidney and Bacon Kebabs with Red Pepper Sauce (bottom).**

ingredients in a deep bowl, cover the bowl loosely and cook 3 minutes on HIGH. Stir the sauce frequently to break up the tomatoes. If desired, blend the sauce until smooth in a food processor. Heat a browning dish for 3 minutes on HIGH. Pour in the oil and add the meat, breaking it up with a fork. Add the garlic and cumin and cook on HIGH for 3 minutes, breaking up the meat frequently. Add the green pepper and cook a further

minute on HIGH. Add the olives, salt and pepper. Roll up the filling in the tortillas and lay them in a shallow casserole, seam side down. Pour over the sauce and cook, uncovered, 1 minute on HIGH to heat through. Top with the avocado slices and cheese and heat 1 minute further on HIGH to melt the cheese.

## Pepper Steak

**PREPARATION TIME:** 20 minutes

**MICROWAVE COOKING TIME:** 14 minutes

**SERVES:** 4 people

1 green pepper, sliced
1 red pepper, sliced
1 yellow pepper, sliced
900g/2lbs rump steak, cut in thin strips
30ml/2 tbsps oil
1 large onion, finely sliced
1 clove garlic
30ml/2 tbsps cornstarch/cornflour
30ml/2 tbsps soy sauce
30ml/2 tbsps dry sherry
430ml/¾ pint/1½ cups beef stock
1 small piece ginger root, grated
Salt and pepper

Heat a browning dish for 5 minutes on HIGH. Pour in the oil and add the strips of steak. Cook 2 minutes on HIGH. Add the onion, garlic and pepper slices. Mix the cornstarch/cornflour and the remaining ingredients and pour over the steak. Cook, uncovered, 7 minutes on HIGH or until the meat is cooked but the vegetables are still crisp. Serve with rice or chow mein noodles.

## Filet Mignon with Mustard Peppercorn Hollandaise

**PREPARATION TIME:** 15 minutes

**MICROWAVE COOKING TIME:**
Steak 9 minutes rare
          10 minutes medium rare
          12 minutes medium
          14 minutes well done
Sauce 2 minutes

**SERVES:** 4 people

4 filet mignon/fillet steaks cut 7.5cms/1½ inches thick, brushed with oil on both sides

**SAUCE**
3 egg yolks
5ml/1 tbsp white wine vinegar
120g/4oz/½ cup butter
15ml/1 tbsp Dijon mustard
5ml/1 tsp green peppercorns
5ml/1 tsp chopped parsley
Salt and pepper

Heat a browning dish 5 minutes on HIGH. Cook the steak 2 minutes on one side and 2½ on the other for rare. For medium rare – 2 minutes on one side and 3½ minutes on the other. For medium – 3 minutes on one side and 4½ minutes on the other. For well done – 3 minutes on one side and 6 minutes on the other. Melt the butter 1 minute on HIGH. Mix the egg yolks, vinegar, salt and pepper in a glass measuring cup/jug. Beat in the butter and cook 15 seconds on HIGH and stir. Continue until the sauce thickens, about 2 minutes. Stir in the mustard, parsley and peppercorns. Serve with the steaks.

## Kidney and Bacon Kebabs with Red Pepper Sauce

**PREPARATION TIME:** 20 minutes

**MICROWAVE COOKING TIME:**
9 minutes, plus
1 minute standing time

**SERVES:** 4 people

16 kidneys
8 strips bacon/streaky bacon
1 green pepper
60g/2oz/¼ cup butter or margarine

**SAUCE**
30ml/2 tbsps dry mustard
30ml/2 tbsps Worcestershire sauce
30ml/2 tbsps brown sauce/steak sauce
2 large caps pimento
Salt and pepper

Pierce the kidneys 2 or 3 times. Cut the kidneys in half through the middle and remove the cores with scissors. Wrap the kidneys in bacon and thread onto wooden skewers with the green pepper. Melt the butter for 1 minute on HIGH and brush over the kebabs. Blend the sauce ingredients together with any remaining butter in a food processor until smooth. Cook the sauce 2 minutes on HIGH. Put the kebabs on a roasting rack and cook 5 minutes on HIGH, turning once. Leave to stand 1 minute before serving. Brush with the cooking juices before serving with the sauce. Saffron rice may also be served.

## Risotto Stuffed Peppers

**PREPARATION TIME:** 20 minutes

**MICROWAVE COOKING TIME:** 20 minutes

**SERVES:** 4 people

2 large or 4 small red, green or yellow peppers
30ml/2 tbsps oil
1 small onion, chopped
1 clove garlic, minced
120g/4oz/1 cup Italian risotto rice
60g/2oz/½ cup mushrooms
120g/4oz/1 cup roughly chopped salami
60g/2oz/¼ cup chopped black olives
225g/8oz canned tomatoes
1.25ml/¼ tsp basil
1.25ml/¼ tsp oregano
120g/4oz/1 cup mozzarella cheese, grated
Paprika
Salt and pepper

In a large casserole, cook the garlic, onion and mushrooms in the oil for 2 minutes on HIGH. Stir in the tomatoes, rice, herbs, salt and pepper. Cover the dish and cook on HIGH for 5 minutes. Stir in the meat and olives and leave to stand 5 minutes for the rice to continue cooking. If the peppers are small, cut 2.5cm/1 inch off the top to form a lid. Remove the core and seeds. If the peppers are large, cut in half lengthwise and remove the core and

**Facing page: Filet Mignon with Mustard Peppercorn Hollandaise (top) and Pepper Steak (bottom).**

seeds. Fill the peppers and place them in the casserole. Cover with plastic wrap/cling film and cook 8 minutes on HIGH, until the peppers are just tender. Top with the cheese and cook 2 minutes on MEDIUM to melt.

## Veal Kidneys in Mustard Sauce

**PREPARATION TIME:** 20 minutes

**MICROWAVE COOKING TIME:** 12 minutes

**SERVES:** 4 people

*2 veal kidneys*
*2 shallots, chopped*
*45g/1½ oz/3 tbsps butter or margarine*
*45g/1½ oz/3 tbsps flour*
*30ml/2 tbsps Dijon mustard*
*140ml/¼ pint/½ cup stock*
*140ml/¼ pint/½ cup light/single cream*
*140ml/¼ pint/½ cup dry white wine*
*15ml/1 tbsp capers*
*15ml/1 tbsp chopped chives*
*Salt and pepper*

Remove the core from the kidneys and cut them into small pieces. Heat a browning dish for 5 minutes on HIGH. Melt the butter for 1 minute on HIGH and add the kidneys and the shallots. Cook 2 minutes on HIGH, stirring frequently. Add the flour, wine, stock, salt and pepper and cook a further 3 minutes on HIGH. Add the remaining ingredients and cook 2 minutes on HIGH. Serve immediately.

## Sherried Sweetbreads

**PREPARATION TIME:** 20 minutes

**MICROWAVE COOKING TIME:** 17 minutes

**SERVES:** 4 people

*450g/1lb lamb or veal sweetbreads, soaked in cold water*
*140ml/¼ pint/½ cup stock*
*60ml/4 tbsps/¼ cup dry sherry*
*120g/4oz mushrooms, sliced*
*220g/8oz small onions, peeled*
*60ml/4 tbsps/¼ cup heavy/double cream*

*Grated nutmeg*
*15ml/1 tbsp tomato purée/paste*
*30ml/2 tbsps chopped parsley*
*Salt and pepper*

Drain the sweetbreads and pierce several times. Cover with fresh water and cook 3 minutes on HIGH. Drain and allow to cool slightly. Peel the outer membrane off the sweetbreads. Cut the sweetbreads in half if they are large. Put the sweetbreads into a casserole with the onions, mushrooms, sherry, stock, salt, pepper and nutmeg. Cook 8 minutes

**This page: Sherried Sweetbreads (top) and Veal Kidneys in Mustard Sauce (bottom). Facing page: Roast Beef with Stuffed Courgettes/Zucchini and Tomatoes (bottom).**

on HIGH, or until tender. Remove the onions, mushrooms and sweetbreads. Cook the liquid until well reduced, about 5 minutes on HIGH. Add the cream and tomato purée/paste and cook 1 minute on HIGH. Mix all the ingredients together in the sauce. Serve with rice or in puff pastry shells.

## Chicken Livers and Walnut Pasta

**PREPARATION TIME:** 15 minutes

**MICROWAVE COOKING TIME:**
13 minutes

**SERVES:** 4 people

450g/1lb chicken livers, trimmed and
    pierced
60g/2oz/¼ cup butter or margarine
1 clove garlic
120g/4oz/½ cup walnuts, roughly
    chopped
280ml/½ pint/1 cup stock
4 spring/green onions
30ml/2 tbsps chopped parsley
1 red pepper, chopped
30ml/2 tbsps sherry
Salt and pepper
225g/8oz pasta, cooked

Heat a browning dish for 5 minutes
on HIGH. Melt the butter for
1 minute on HIGH and add the liver.
Cook for 2 minutes on HIGH and
add the garlic, salt and pepper and
stock. Cook 3 minutes on HIGH.
Remove the livers from the stock and
pour the stock into a food processor.
Add the walnuts and blend until
smooth. Chop the green/spring
onions and add to the sauce with the
parsley, red peppers, and sherry. Pour
over the livers and heat 2 minutes on
HIGH. Pour over pasta to serve.

## Roast Beef with Stuffed Courgettes/Zucchini and Tomatoes

**PREPARATION TIME:** 20 minutes

**MICROWAVE COOKING TIME:**
Beef 14-21 minutes – rare
      16-24 minutes – medium
      18-27 minutes – well done
plus 10 minutes standing time

**COMBINATION MICROWAVE
CONVECTION TIME:**
Beef 10-12 minutes – rare
      11-13 minutes – medium
      12-14 minutes – well done
Vegetables 13 minutes

**SERVES:** 6-8 people

900g-1.5kg/2-3lbs boneless beef roast/
    joint
6-8 tomatoes
6-8 courgettes/zucchini
60ml/4 tbsps chopped parsley
180g/6oz mushrooms, roughly chopped
60ml/4 tbsps chopped chives
60g/2oz/½ cup breadcrumbs
60g/2oz/1 cup grated cheese
Salt and pepper

Put the beef, fat side up, into a large
casserole, cover loosely and cook for
14-21 minutes for rare, 16-24 minutes
for medium, 18-27 minutes for well
done on HIGH. Turn the beef over
halfway through the cooking time.
When cooked for the chosen amount
of time cover with foil and leave to
stand for 10 minutes before carving.
The beef may also be cooked in a
combination microwave and
convection oven. Trim the ends of
the courgettes/zucchini and cook, in
enough water to cover, for 5 minutes
on HIGH. Cut in half lengthwise and
scoop out the flesh, leaving the shell
intact. Chop the flesh roughly and
mix with the chives, salt and pepper.
Fill the shells and sprinkle on the
grated cheese. Cut the tops from the
round end of the tomatoes, scoop
out the seeds and strain the juice.
Mix the mushrooms, tomato juice,
parsley, breadcrumbs, salt and
pepper. Fill the tomatoes and replace
the tops. Cook the courgettes/
zucchini 5 minutes on HIGH and the
tomatoes 3 minutes on HIGH, or
until the vegetables are tender. Serve
with the beef.

## Beef Bourguignonne

**PREPARATION TIME:** 20 minutes

**MICROWAVE COOKING TIME:**
53 minutes, plus
10 minutes standing time

**SERVES:** 4 people

2 thick-cut slices bacon cut in 1.25cm/
    ½ inch strips
675g-900g/1½lbs-2lbs chuck/braising
    steak cut in 2.5cm/1 inch cubes
1 clove garlic, minced
225g/8oz small onions
60g/4 tbsps flour/plain flour

280ml/½ pint/1 cup Burgundy
280ml/½ pint/1 cup beef stock
5ml/1 tsp tomato paste/purée
225g/8oz mushrooms, left whole
1 bay leaf
5ml/1 tsp thyme or majoram
Salt and pepper

Heat a browning dish for 5 minutes
on HIGH. Add the bacon and cook
3 minutes on HIGH, stirring
frequently until brown. Remove the
bacon and add the meat. Cook 3
minutes on HIGH to brown slightly.
Remove the meat and add the
onions. Cook 2 minutes on HIGH.
Stir in the flour, stock, wine and
tomato purée/paste. Add the bay
leaf, salt and pepper. Return the
bacon and meat to the casserole and
add the mushrooms. Cover and cook
40 minutes on MEDIUM, or until
the meat is tender. Stir occasionally.
Leave to stand for 10 minutes before
serving. Serve with parsley potatoes.

## Steak and Mushroom Pudding

**PREPARATION TIME:** 25 minutes

**MICROWAVE COOKING TIME:**
51-52 minutes, plus
10 minutes standing time

**SERVES:** 4 people

**PASTRY**
225g/8oz/2 cups flour/plain flour
10ml/2 tsps baking powder
120g/4oz shredded suet or ¼ cup butter or
    margarine
5ml/1 tsp salt
140ml/¼ pint/½ cup water

**FILLING**
225g/8oz whole mushrooms
450g/1lb braising/chuck steak
30g/1oz/2 tbsps butter or margarine
30g/1oz/2 tbsps flour
1 small onion, finely chopped
280ml/½ pint/1 cup beef stock
10ml/2 tsps chopped parsley
5ml/1 tsp thyme
Salt and pepper

**Facing page: Steak and Mushroom
Pudding (top) and Beef
Bourguignonne (bottom).**

Melt the butter in a deep bowl for 30 seconds on HIGH. Stir in the flour and the stock and cook for 1-2 minutes on HIGH. Add the remaining ingredients for the filling and cover the bowl loosely. Cook for 35 minutes on MEDIUM. Meanwhile, make the pastry. Sift the flour and baking powder and salt into a mixing bowl. Cut in the butter or stir in the suet. Mix to a soft dough with the water. Roll out ⅔ of the dough and line a 1150ml/2 pint/ 4 cup glass bowl, spoon in the filling and dampen the edges of the pastry. Roll out the remaining pastry for the cover. Place it over the top of the filling, pressing down the edges to seal well. Make 2-3 cuts in the top to let out the steam. Cover loosely with plastic wrap/cling film and cook on LOW for 15 minutes, turning the bowl around several times. Leave to stand for 10 minutes before turning out.

## Veal Escalopes with Vegetables

**PREPARATION TIME:** 20 minutes

**MICROWAVE COOKING TIME:** 20 minutes

**SERVES:** 4 people

*4 veal escalopes/cutlets*
*30ml/2 tbsps oil*
*60g/2oz mangetout/peapods*
*2 carrots, peeled and thinly sliced*
*60g/2oz mushrooms, sliced*
*2 leeks, washed and thinly sliced*
*120g/4oz/1 cup low-fat soft cheese*
*140ml/¼ pint/½ cup dry white wine*
*15ml/1 tbsp lemon juice*
*15ml/1 tbsp chopped dill*
*Grated nutmeg*
*Salt and pepper*

Heat a browning dish 3 minutes on HIGH. Add the oil and heat 1 minute on HIGH. Cook the veal for 8 minutes on HIGH. Add the mushrooms halfway through the cooking time. Combine the carrots and the leeks with the wine in a shallow dish and cook for 5 minutes on HIGH. Add the mangetout/ peapods and cook a further 1 minute

on HIGH. Drain the vegetables and reserve the liquid. Mix the cheese, vegetable cooking liquid, lemon juice, dill, nutmeg, salt and pepper in a deep bowl. Heat for 1 minute on HIGH, but do not allow the sauce to boil. Combine with the drained vegetables. Pour over the veal and heat through 1 minute on HIGH before serving.

## Veal with Saffron Sauce

**PREPARATION TIME:** 20 minutes

**MICROWAVE COOKING TIME:** 26-27 minutes

**SERVES:** 4 people

*4 veal chops*
*45g/1½ oz/3 tbsps butter or margarine*
*30g/1oz/2 tbsps flour/plain flour*
*2 shallots, finely chopped*
*1 red pepper, thinly sliced*
*140ml/¼ pint/½ cup white wine*
*140ml/¼ pint/½ cup light stock*
*140ml/¼ pint/½ cup light/single cream*
*Good pinch saffron*
*Salt and pepper*

Heat a browning dish for 5 minutes on HIGH. Melt the butter for 1 minute on HIGH and put in the chops. Cook for 2 minutes on HIGH per side. Remove the chops from the dish and add the shallots. Cook for 1 minute on HIGH. Stir in the flour, wine, stock, salt, pepper and saffron.

Cook 2-3 minutes on HIGH until thickened. Return the chops to the dish and add the sliced red pepper. Cover the dish or transfer to a covered casserole. Cook on MEDIUM for 15 minutes, or until the chops are tender. Remove the chops from the dish and stir in the cream. Pour the sauce over the chops to serve.

## Veal Chops with Lemon and Thyme

**PREPARATION TIME:** 20 minutes

**MICROWAVE COOKING TIME:** 26-27 minutes

**SERVES:** 4 people

*4 veal chops*
*60g/2oz/¼ cup butter or margarine*
*60g/2oz/¼ cup flour*
*1 clove garlic, minced*
*140ml/¼ pint/½ cup white wine*
*140ml/¼ pint/½ cup light stock*
*30ml/2 tbsps lemon juice*
*Salt and pepper*

**GARNISH**
*Sprigs of fresh thyme*
*Lemon slices*

Heat a browning dish 5 minutes on HIGH. Melt the butter for 1 minute on HIGH. Put in the chops and cook 2 minutes on HIGH per side.

**Facing page: Veal Chops with Lemon and Thyme (top) and Veal with Saffron Sauce (bottom). This page: Veal Escalopes with Vegetables.**

Remove the chops from the dish and add the flour. Cook 1 minute to brown slightly. Stir in the wine, stock and lemon juice. Cook 2-3 minutes on HIGH until thickened. Season with salt and pepper and add a sprig of fresh thyme. Return the chops to the dish or transfer to a covered casserole. Cook on MEDIUM 15 minutes. Garnish with lemon slices and more fresh thyme.

# POULTRY DISHES

## Orange Glazed Duck

**PREPARATION TIME:** 15 minutes

**MICROWAVE COOKING TIME:**
40 minutes

**SERVES:** 3-4 people

2kg-2.5kg/4½-5lbs duckling
1 slice orange
1 slice onion
1 bay leaf
Salt

**GLAZE**
60ml/4 tbsps/¼ cup bitter orange
   marmalade
60ml/4 tbsps soy sauce
280ml/½ pint/1 cup chicken stock
10ml/2 tsps cornstarch/cornflour
Salt and pepper

**GARNISH**
Orange slices and watercress

Prick the duck all over the skin with a fork, brush some of the soy sauce over both sides of the duck and sprinkle both sides lightly with salt. Place the duck breast side down in a roasting rack. Cook 10 minutes on HIGH and drain well. Return the duckling to the oven, reduce the power to MEDIUM and continue cooking a further 15 minutes. Combine remaining soy sauce with the orange marmalade. Turn the duck breast side up and brush with the glaze. Continue cooking for 15 minutes on MEDIUM, draining away the fat often and brushing with the glaze. Remove the duck from the roasting rack and leave to stand, loosely covered with foil, for 5 minutes before carving. Alternatively, cook 20-25 minutes on Combination in a microwave convection oven. Drain all the fat from the roasting tin, but leave the pan juices. Combine the chicken stock, cornstarch/cornflour, salt, pepper and remaining glaze with the

**This page: Orange Glazed Duck.
Facing page: Turkey with Broccoli
(top) and Turkey Tetrazzini
(bottom).**

## Stuffed Turkey Leg

**PREPARATION TIME:** 20 minutes

**MICROWAVE COOKING TIME:** 33-34 minutes

**SERVES:** 4 people

*1 large turkey leg, bone removed*

**STUFFING**
*2 slices white bread made into crumbs*
*120g/4oz cooked ham, finely minced*
*60g/2oz/½ cup shelled pistachio nuts*
*1 apple, cored and chopped*
*2 sticks celery, finely chopped*
*1 shallot, finely chopped*
*Pinch thyme*
*1 egg, beaten*
*Salt and pepper*

**SAUCE**
*15ml/1 tbsp dripping from turkey*
*30g/2 tbsps flour/plain flour*
*Pan juices*
*280ml/½ pint/1 cup chicken stock*
*30ml/2 tbsps dry sherry*
*Salt and pepper*

**GARNISH**
*1 bunch watercress*

Combine all the stuffing ingredients and push into the cavity of the turkey leg, but do not overstuff. Close any openings with wooden picks/cocktail sticks. Prick the turkey skin lightly all over and put the turkey leg on a roasting rack. Cover loosely with greaseproof/wax paper and cook for 15 minutes on MEDIUM. Turn the turkey leg over and continue cooking on MEDIUM a further 15 minutes. Alternatively, cook 20 minutes on Combination in a microwave convection oven. When the turkey is tender and no longer pink, remove from the roasting rack and keep warm. Remove all but 15ml/1 tbsp of the fat from the roasting dish. Stir in the flour and add the chicken stock, sherry, salt and pepper. Transfer to a deep bowl if

pan juices and pour into a small, deep bowl. Cook 2-3 minutes on HIGH until thickened. Remove the onion, orange slice and bay leaf from the cavity of the duck and put in a bouquet of watercress. Surround the duck with orange slices and serve the sauce separately.

## Lemon Pepper Chicken

**PREPARATION TIME:** 20 minutes

**MICROWAVE COOKING TIME:** 10 minutes

**SERVES:** 4 people

*4 chicken breasts*
*Juice of 1 lemon*
*15ml/1 tbsp coarsely ground black pepper*

*Paprika*
*Salt*

**GARNISH**
*Lemon slices*
*Watercress*

Heat 2 metal skewers in a gas flame or on an electric burner/hob. Skin the chicken breasts. Make a criss-cross pattern on the chicken flesh with the hot skewers. Place the chicken in a casserole and sprinkle over the paprika, pepper, lemon juice and salt. Cover the dish tightly and cook 10 minutes on MEDIUM. Pour the juices back over the chicken to serve. Garnish with the lemon slices and watercress.

**This page: Stuffed Turkey Leg. Facing page: Lemon Pepper Chicken (top) and Lime and Chili Chicken (bottom).**

desired and cook 3-4 minutes on HIGH, stirring frequently until thickened. Slice the stuffed turkey leg and pour over some of the sauce. Garnish with watercress and serve the remaining sauce separately.

## Chinese Wings

**PREPARATION TIME:** 15 minutes

**MICROWAVE COOKING TIME:** 17 minutes

**SERVES:** 4 people

1.5kg/3lbs chicken wings
280ml/½ pint/1 cup hoisin sauce
   (Chinese barbecue sauce)
45g/1½ oz/3 tbsps sesame seeds
30ml/2 tbsps vegetable oil
15ml/1 tbsp sesame seed oil
225g/8oz mangetout/peapods
225g/8oz bean sprouts
Small piece grated fresh ginger root
Salt and pepper

Brush the chicken wings with the hoisin sauce and cook for 10 minutes on HIGH on a roasting rack. Baste the chicken wings often with the sauce while cooking. When the wings are cooked and well coated with sauce, sprinkle with sesame seeds and set aside. Heat the oil in a browning dish for 5 minutes on HIGH. Add the mangetout/peapods, bean sprouts, ginger, salt and pepper. Cook for 2 minutes on HIGH and add the sesame seed oil after cooking. Serve the Chinese wings with the stir-fried vegetables.

## Lime and Chili Chicken

**PREPARATION TIME:** 20 minutes

**MICROWAVE COOKING TIME:** 12 minutes

**SERVES:** 4 people

4 chicken breasts, boned
2 limes
1 green chili pepper
90ml/6 tbsps/⅓ cup heavy/double
   cream
Salt and pepper
Pinch sugar

Heat 2 metal skewers in a gas flame or on an electric hob/burner. Skin the chicken breasts and make a pattern on the chicken flesh with the hot skewers. Squeeze 1 lime for juice. Peel and slice the other lime thinly. Remove the seeds from the chili pepper and slice it very thinly. Put the chicken into a casserole. Sprinkle over a pinch of sugar, the sliced chili pepper, salt, pepper and lime juice. Cover and cook 10 minutes on MEDIUM. Remove the chicken and keep warm. Stir the cream into the juices in the casserole. Cook 2 minutes on HIGH, stirring frequently. Pour over the chicken and garnish with the sliced lime.

## Tandoori Poussins

**PREPARATION TIME:** 20 minutes, plus 1 hour to marinate

**MICROWAVE COOKING TIME:** 15 minutes

**SERVES:** 4 people

4 poussins

**MARINADE**
120g/4oz/½ cup chopped onion
1 small piece fresh ginger, grated
10ml/2 tsps ground coriander
10ml/2 tsps ground cumin
10ml/2 tsps paprika
5ml/1 tsp turmeric
5ml/1 tsp chili powder
280ml/½ pint/1 cup plain yogurt
Juice of 1 lime
2 chopped green chili peppers
30ml/2 tbsps chopped chives
Salt and pepper

**ACCOMPANIMENT**
1 head of lettuce, broken into leaves
4 tomatoes, cut in wedges
1 lemon, cut in wedges

Combine all the marinade ingredients together. Skin the poussins and cut them in half. Prick the flesh and rub in the marinade. Leave for 1 hour. Cook on HIGH or a Combination setting for 15 minutes, basting frequently with the marinade. Leave to stand, loosely covered, for 5 minutes before

serving. Heat any remaining marinade on MEDIUM for 1 minute, but do not allow to boil. Pour over the chicken and serve on a bed of lettuce with lemon and tomato wedges.

## Turkey with Broccoli

**PREPARATION TIME:** 20 minutes

**MICROWAVE COOKING TIME:** 13-14 minutes

**SERVES:** 4 people

4 turkey escalopes/cutlets
12 broccoli spears
140ml/¼ pint/½ cup chicken stock
1 bay leaf
Salt and pepper

**SAUCE**
45g/3 tbsps butter or margarine
45g/3 tbsps flour/plain flour
430ml/¾ pint/1½ cups milk
60g/2oz/½ cup Colby/Red Leicester
   cheese
Pinch Cayenne pepper
Salt and pepper
Paprika

Trim the broccoli, and divide evenly among the turkey escalopes/cutlets. Roll the turkey around the broccoli and lay the rolls in a casserole, seam side down. Pour over the chicken stock, sprinkle on salt and pepper and add the bay leaf. Cover and cook 10 minutes on MEDIUM. Leave to stand while preparing the sauce. Melt the butter for 30 seconds in a deep bowl. Stir in the flour and the milk. Add the salt, pepper, mustard, Cayenne pepper and cook until thickened, about 3-4 minutes on HIGH. Add the cheese and stir to melt. Transfer the turkey and broccoli rolls to a serving dish and pour some of the sauce over each one. Sprinkle on paprika and serve the rest of the sauce separately.

**Facing page: Chinese Wings (top) and Tandoori Poussins (bottom).**

## Herb Roasted Chicken

**PREPARATION TIME:** 25 minutes

**MICROWAVE COOKING TIME:**
26-33 minutes, plus
5-10 minutes standing time

**SERVES:** 4-6 people

1.5kg/3lbs roasting chicken
5ml/1 tsp each fresh thyme, basil, parsley,
    marjoram, chervil or tarragon
30ml/2 tbsps oil
Juice of 1 lemon
Salt and pepper

**GRAVY**
45g/1½ oz/3 tbsps flour/plain flour
Cooking juices from the chicken
430ml/¾ pint/1½ cups chicken stock
30ml/2 tbsps white wine
30ml/2 tbsps chopped mixed herbs as
    above
Salt and pepper

Chop the herbs finely. Loosen the skin of the chicken and stuff the herbs underneath. Prick the skin lightly and brush with the oil. Sprinkle over the lemon juice and pepper. Put onto a roasting rack breast-side down, and cook 30 minutes on MEDIUM, 25 minutes on HIGH and 30 minutes on a Combination setting. Turn the chicken halfway through cooking. Leave the chicken standing 5-10 minutes before carving. If the chicken appears to be drying out at any time during cooking, baste with oil and cover loosely with wax paper/greaseproof paper. Reserve 1 tbsp fat from the roasting pan and skim off the rest and discard. Reserve the pan juices. Mix the reserved fat with the flour and stir into the pan juices. Add the stock, wine, salt and pepper and cook 2-3 minutes until thickened. Stir in the chopped herbs and serve with the carved chicken.

## Duck with Peaches

**PREPARATION TIME:** 20 minutes

**MICROWAVE COOKING TIME:**
9 minutes

**SERVES:** 4 people

2 whole duck breasts
60g/4 tbsps/¼ cup butter
Salt and pepper

**SAUCE**
2 cans sliced peaches, drained and juice
    reserved
140ml/¼ pint/½ cup red wine
10ml/2 tsps cornstarch/cornflour
15ml/1 tbsp lime or lemon juice
1 bay leaf
Pinch cinnamon
Pinch nutmeg
15ml/1 tbsp whole allspice berries
60g/2oz/½ cup whole blanched almonds

Heat a browning dish for 5 minutes on HIGH. Melt the butter and put in the duck breasts. Brown the duck breasts 2 minutes on the skin side and 4 minutes on the other side. Remove from the dish and leave to stand while preparing the sauce. Mix the cornstarch/cornflour with the peach juice, red wine, lemon juice and the spices and bay leaf in a deep bowl. Cook on HIGH for 2-3 minutes until thickened. Remove the bay leaf and add the peaches. Slice the duck breast into thin slices. Pour the peach sauce over the duck breasts to serve.

**This page: Herb Roasted Chicken.
Facing page: Turkey Macadamia
(top) and Duck with Peaches
(bottom).**

## Spicy Tomato Chicken

**PREPARATION TIME:** 15 minutes

**MICROWAVE COOKING TIME:**
17 minutes, plus
5 minutes standing time

**SERVES:** 4 people

4 chicken breasts, skinned and boned
60ml/4 tbsps/¼ cup chicken stock or
    water
450g/1lb canned tomatoes
30ml/2 tbsps Worcestershire sauce
1 clove garlic, crushed
30ml/2 tbsps tomato purée/paste
30ml/2 tbsps cider vinegar
30g/1oz/2 tbsps light brown sugar or
    honey
1 small onion, finely chopped
1 bay leaf
Pinch allspice
Salt and pepper
**GARNISH**
4 tomatoes, skinned, seeded and cut into
    thin strips

Place the chicken in 1 layer in a large
casserole with the stock or water.
Cover tightly and cook on
MEDIUM for 10 minutes. Leave to
stand, covered, for at least 5 minutes
while preparing the sauce. Combine
all the sauce ingredients with the
cooking liquid from the chicken in a
deep bowl. Cook, uncovered, for
7 minutes on HIGH, until the sauce
reduces and thickens. Remove the
bay leaf and blend the sauce in a food
processor until smooth. Arrange the
chicken breasts on a serving plate
and coat with the sauce. Add the
tomato strips and reheat for
30 seconds on HIGH before serving.

## Chicken with Watercress Sauce

**PREPARATION TIME:** 15 minutes

**MICROWAVE COOKING TIME:**
12 minutes, plus
5 minutes standing time

**SERVES:** 4 people

4 large chicken breasts, skinned and
    boned
30ml/2 tbsps water
60ml/4 tbsps/¼ cup lemon juice

**SAUCE**
120g/4oz/1 cup low fat soft cheese
140ml/¼ pint/½ cup light/single cream
    or milk
1 large bunch watercress, well washed
    and drained
Salt and pepper
**GARNISH**
Lemon slices
Watercress

Place the chicken in one layer in a
large casserole. Pour over the water
and the lemon juice. Cover tightly
and cook 10 minutes on MEDIUM.
Leave to stand, covered, at least
5 minutes while preparing the sauce.
Combine the cheese and the cream
or milk with the chicken cooking
liquid and salt and pepper. Cook
1 minute on HIGH. Discard any
tough stalks from the watercress and
chop roughly. Add to the sauce and
cook 1 minute on HIGH. Blend the
sauce in a food processor until
smooth and a delicate green colour.
Coat over the chicken to serve.
Garnish with lemon slices and
watercress.

**This page: Country Captain's
Chicken. Facing page: Chicken
with Watercress Sauce (top) and
Spicy Tomato Chicken (bottom).**

## Country Captain's Chicken

**PREPARATION TIME:** 20 minutes

**MICROWAVE COOKING TIME:**
36 minutes

**SERVES:** 4 people

1.5kg/3lbs chicken pieces
60g/4 tbsps butter
30ml/2 tbsps curry powder
1 clove garlic, minced
1 large onion, sliced
60g/2oz/½ cup blanched whole almonds
60g/2oz/½ cup golden raisins/sultanas
2 apples, peeled and diced
1 450g/16oz can tomatoes
30ml/2 tbsps tomato purée/paste
1 bay leaf
30ml/2 tbsps chopped coriander
    (optional)
Pinch sugar
Salt and pepper

**GARNISH**
*Desiccated coconut*

Heat a browning dish for 5 minutes on HIGH. Melt the butter and add the chicken pieces. Cook 15 minutes on both sides or cook in 2 batches for 7½ minutes each batch if necessary. Remove the chicken and add the onion, garlic and curry powder. Cook 1 minute on HIGH. Replace the chicken, skin side down, and add the sultanas/raisins, apples and almonds. Mix the tomatoes, tomato purée/paste, lime juice, coriander, bay leaf, sugar, salt and pepper together and pour over the chicken. Cook 15 minutes on HIGH, or until the chicken is tender and no longer pink. Turn the chicken over halfway through cooking. Remove the bay leaf and serve with rice and garnish with desiccated coconut.

## Piquant Duck

**PREPARATION TIME:** 25 minutes

**MICROWAVE COOKING TIME:** 27 minutes

**SERVES:** 4 people

*8 duck portions/pieces*
*60g/2oz/¼ cup butter*
*4 large cloves garlic, minced*

**SAUCE**
*60ml/2 fl oz/¼ cup vinegar*
*280ml/½ pint/1 cup dry white wine*
*45ml/3 tbsps Dijon mustard*
*30ml/2 tbsps tomato purée/paste*
*30ml/2 tbsps chives*
*1 red pepper, very thinly sliced*
*140ml/¼ pint/½ cup heavy/double cream*
*Salt and pepper*

Heat a browning dish for 5 minutes on HIGH, melt the butter and add the duck pieces skin side down. Brown the duck for 5 minutes per side. Add the garlic and cover the dish tightly. Cook until the duck is tender, about 15 minutes on HIGH. Pour off all the fat and leave the duck covered while preparing the sauce. Combine all the sauce ingredients except the red pepper and the cream in a deep bowl. Add the garlic and any juices from the duck. Cook for 10 minutes on HIGH until well reduced. Add the cream and the red pepper and cook a further 2 minutes on HIGH. Trim the duck pieces neatly and pour over the sauce to serve.

## Turkey Macadamia

**PREPARATION TIME:** 20 minutes

**MICROWAVE COOKING TIME:** 18 minutes

**SERVES:** 4 people

*4 turkey breast escalopes/cutlets*
*1 225g (8oz) can pineapple chunks/ pieces, juice reserved*
*4 spring/green onions, sliced*
*4 tomatoes, peeled, seeded and quartered*
*125g/4oz/1 cup macadamia nuts*

**SAUCE**
*30ml/2 tbsps soy sauce*
*280ml/½ pint/1 cup stock*
*30ml/2 tbsps vinegar*
*30ml/2 tbsps brown sugar*
*15ml/3 tsps cornstarch/cornflour*
*Reserved pineapple juice*

Place the turkey breasts in a casserole dish and pour over the pineapple juice. Cover the dish tightly and cook 10-15 minutes on MEDIUM. Leave to stand while preparing the sauce. Drain the pineapple juice from the turkey and combine it in a deep bowl with the remaining sauce ingredients. Add the pineapple pieces and the macadamia nuts. Cook, uncovered, for 2-3 minutes on HIGH, stirring frequently until thickened. Immediately add the tomatoes and the onions to the hot sauce and pour over the turkey to serve.

## Turkey Tetrazzini

**PREPARATION TIME:** 20 minutes

**MICROWAVE COOKING TIME:** 6-8 minutes

**SERVES:** 4-6 people

*60g/2oz/¼ cup butter or margarine*
*60g/2oz flour/plain flour*
*120g/4oz mushrooms, sliced*
*1 clove garlic, crushed*
*2 sticks celery, sliced*
*280ml/½ pint/1 cup chicken stock*
*280ml/½ pint/1 cup milk*
*140ml/¼ pint/½ cup double/heavy cream*
*30ml/2 tbsps dry white wine or sherry*
*12 black olives, pitted and roughly chopped*
*225g/8oz cooked turkey, cut in cubes*
*225g/8oz spaghetti*
*Salt and pepper*
*60g/4 tbsps/¼ cup each seasoned breadcrumbs and Parmesan cheese*

Cook spaghetti in enough water to cover for 12 minutes on HIGH. Stir frequently. Drain and set aside. Melt the butter 30 seconds on HIGH, and add mushrooms, garlic and celery. Cook 1 minute on HIGH. Stir in the flour and add milk, stock and wine or sherry. Cook, uncovered, until thickened, about 5 minutes on HIGH. Add the cream and the olives. Combine with the turkey and spaghetti and pour into a casserole. Sprinkle cheese and crumbs on top and cook 8-10 minutes on HIGH. Serve immediately.

## Duck with Cherries

**PREPARATION TIME:** 20 minutes

**MICROWAVE COOKING TIME:** 9 minutes

**SERVES:** 4 people

*2 whole duck breasts*
*60g/4 tbsps/¼ cup butter or margarine*
*Salt and pepper*

**SAUCE**
*2 cans dark, pitted cherries, drained and juice reserved*
*140ml/¼ pint/½ cup red wine*
*30ml/2 tbsps red wine vinegar*
*Grated rind and juice of 1 orange*
*10ml/2 tsps cornstarch/cornflour*
*1 bay leaf*
*1 sprig thyme*
*Pinch salt*

**Facing page:** Duck with Cherries (top) and Piquant Duck (bottom).

Heat a browning dish 5 minutes on HIGH. Add the butter and put in the duck breasts. Brown the duck breasts 2 minutes on the skin side and 4 minutes on the other side. Remove the duck from the dish and keep warm. Mix the reserved cherry juice with the wine, vinegar, orange rind and juice, cornstarch/cornflour, bay leaf and thyme in a small bowl. Cook for 3 minutes on HIGH until thickened, stirring frequently. Add a pinch of salt and remove the bay leaf and thyme. Add the cherries to the sauce and slice the duck breasts into thin slices. Pour over the cherry sauce to serve.

## Pecan Poussins

**PREPARATION TIME:** 25 minutes

**MICROWAVE COOKING TIME:** 35 minutes

**SERVES:** 4 people

4 poussins or Cornish game hens
60ml/4 tbsps/¼ cup Worcestershire
  sauce

**STUFFING**
6 slices white bread made into crumbs
225g/8oz cooked ham
4 green/spring onions, chopped
5ml/1 tsp thyme
1 egg, beaten
Salt and pepper

**SAUCE**
430ml/¾ pint/1½ cups brown stock
180g/6oz/⅔ cup light brown sugar
90ml/6 tbsps/⅓ cup cider vinegar
120g/4oz/1 cup chopped pecans

**GARNISH**
Watercress

Process the ham and bread in a food processor until finely chopped. Add the egg, salt, pepper and thyme and process once or twice to mix thoroughly. Stir in the onion by hand. Stuff the poussins and tie the legs together with string. Brush each poussin with Worcestershire sauce. Cook 15-20 minutes on HIGH or 20 minutes on a Combination setting. Leave to stand 5 minutes

before serving. Mix the sauce ingredients together and cook on HIGH, uncovered, for 10-15 minutes. The sauce should be reduced and of syrupy consistency. Pour over the poussins to serve and garnish with watercress.

## Chicken Paprika

**PREPARATION TIME:** 20 minutes

**MICROWAVE COOKING TIME:** 32 minutes, plus 5 minutes standing time

**SERVES:** 4-6 people

1.5kg/3lbs chicken pieces
30g/1oz/2 tbsps butter
2 onions, sliced
30ml/2 tbsps paprika
1 clove garlic, finely minced
30ml/2 tbsps tomato purée/paste
1 450g/1lb can tomatoes
120g/4oz mushrooms
1 green pepper, thinly sliced
1 bay leaf
Salt and pepper

**This page: Chicken Paprika.
Facing page: Pecan Poussins.**

**GARNISH**
Sour cream

Melt the butter for 30 seconds on HIGH in a large casserole. Add the paprika, onions and garlic. Cook, uncovered, 2 minutes on HIGH. Lay the chicken pieces into the casserole skin-side down with the thickest portions to the outside of the dish. Combine the tomato paste/purée with the tomatoes, bay leaf, salt and pepper. Pour the tomato sauce over the chicken and cover the casserole tightly. Cook for 15 minutes on HIGH. Turn over the chicken pieces and scatter the mushrooms and the pepper slices on top. Cook a further 15 minutes, or until the chicken is tender and no longer pink. Leave to stand, covered, for 5 minutes. Top with sour cream before serving with pasta or potatoes.

# GAME DISHES

## Quail with Artichokes and Vegetable Julienne

**PREPARATION TIME:** 25 minutes

**MICROWAVE COOKING TIME:** 19-21 minutes

**SERVES:** 4 people

8 quail
60g/4 tbsps/¼ cup butter or margarine
2 large artichokes, cooked
2 carrots, peeled
2 potatoes, peeled
2 leeks, washed

**SAUCE**
15ml/1 tbsps flour/plain flour
140ml/¼ pint/½ cup white wine
280ml/½ pint/1 cup double/heavy
   cream
30ml/2 tbsps Dijon mustard
Salt and pepper

**GARNISH**
Reserved artichoke leaves

Peel the leaves from the artichokes and remove the chokes. Set the leaves aside and cut the artichoke bottoms into thin slices. Cut the carrots, potatoes and leeks into julienne strips. Heat a browning dish for 5 minutes on HIGH. Melt the butter and add the carrots and potatoes. Cook on HIGH for 2 minutes. Add the leeks and artichoke bottoms and cook for a further 1 minute on HIGH. Remove the vegetables and set them aside. Add the quail to the butter in a dish and cook for 4-6 minutes on HIGH, turning frequently to brown lightly. Remove the quail from the dish and add the flour, white wine and Dijon mustard. Return the quail to the

dish, cover tightly and cook for 5 minutes on HIGH. Set the quail aside to keep warm. Add the cream and salt and pepper to the dish and stir well. Cook for 1 minute on HIGH to thicken slightly. Add the vegetables to the sauce and cook a further 1 minute on HIGH to heat

**This page: Quail with Raspberries. Facing page: Quail with Apples and Calvados (top) and Quail with Artichokes and Vegetable Julienne (bottom).**

through. Pour the sauce over the quail to serve and surround with the artichoke leaves.

## Juniper Venison

**PREPARATION TIME:** 25 minutes

**MICROWAVE COOKING TIME:**
55 minutes, plus
10 minutes standing time

**SERVES:** 4 people

*900g/2lbs venison, cut in 2.5cm/1 inch
   cubes*
*60g/2oz/¼ cup butter or margarine*
*60g/2oz/¼ cup flour/plain flour*
*570ml/1 pint/2 cups beef stock*
*60ml/4 tbsps/¼ cup red wine*
*1 shallot, finely chopped*
*1 sprig rosemary*
*15ml/1 tbsp juniper berries*
*1 bay leaf*
*Salt and pepper*

**ACCOMPANIMENT**
*450g/1lb potatoes, peeled and cut into
   small pieces*
*15g/1 tbsp butter or margarine*
*1 egg, beaten*
*Salt and pepper*
*Rowanberry jelly, redcurrant jelly or whole
   cranberry sauce*

Cook the potatoes in enough water
to cover for 15 minutes on HIGH.
Leave to stand for 5 minutes before
draining and mashing. Season the
potatoes with salt and pepper and
add the butter. Beat in half the egg
and pipe the mixture out into small
baskets on a plate or a microwave
baking sheet. Cook for 1 minute on
HIGH and then brush with the
remaining beaten egg and sprinkle
with paprika. Cook a further
2 minutes on HIGH and set aside.
Heat a browning dish for 5 minutes
on HIGH. Melt the butter and
brown the meat and the shallot for
4-6 minutes on HIGH. Remove the
meat and shallot and stir in the flour,
stock, red wine, salt, pepper, juniper
berries, rosemary and bay leaf. Return
the meat to the dish or transfer to a
casserole. Cover and cook for
30 minutes on MEDIUM, stirring
frequently. Remove the bay leaf and
the sprig of rosemary before serving.
Reheat the potato baskets for
30 seconds on HIGH and fill each
with a spoonful of the jelly or
cranberry sauce. Serve the potato

baskets with the venison. Garnish
with fresh rosemary if desired.

## Marmalade Venison

**PREPARATION TIME:** 15 minutes

**MICROWAVE COOKING TIME:**
40 minutes, plus
10 minutes standing time

**SERVES:** 4 people

*900g/2lbs venison, cut in 2.5cm/1 inch
   cubes*
*225g/8oz small onions, peeled and left
   whole*

**This page: Juniper Venison (top)
and Marmalade Venison (bottom).
Facing page: Pheasant Alsacienne.**

*60g/2oz/¼ cup butter or margarine*
*60g/2oz/¼ cup flour*
*570ml/1 pint/2 cups beef stock*
*60ml/4 tbsps/¼ cup orange marmalade*

**GARNISH**
*Orange slices*
*Chopped parsley*

Heat a browning dish for 5 minutes
on HIGH. Melt the butter and add

the venison. Cook 4-6 minutes on HIGH, stirring frequently. Remove the meat and add the onions. Cook 1-2 minutes on HIGH to brown slightly. Remove the onions and add the flour, stock and marmalade. Return the meat and the onions to the casserole, cover and cook 30 minutes on MEDIUM. Leave to stand 10 minutes before serving. Garnish with orange slices and sprinkle with chopped parsley before serving.

## Garlic Roast Pigeon

**PREPARATION TIME:** 20 minutes

**MICROWAVE COOKING TIME:**
15 minutes, plus
5 minutes standing time

**SERVES:** 4 people

4 pigeons
60g/2oz/4 tbsps butter or margarine
12 cloves garlic, peeled
60ml/2 fl oz/¼ cup white wine
280ml/½ pint/1 cup chicken stock
1 bay leaf
1 sprig thyme
Salt and pepper

**ACCOMPANIMENT**
4 heads Belgian endive/chicory
280ml/½ pint/1 cup water and white
    wine mixed
Pinch sugar
Salt and pepper

Spread the butter on the pigeons and place them breast side up on a roasting rack with the cloves of garlic. Cook on HIGH or a Combination setting for 10 minutes. Leave the pigeons to stand for 5 minutes before serving. They may be served slightly pink. Meanwhile, mash the cloves of garlic and mix with the stock, wine, bay leaf and salt and pepper. Cook, uncovered, for 3 minutes to reduce the liquid. Purée the sauce until smooth. Cut the endive/chicory in half lengthwise and remove the cores. Put into a casserole dish with the wine and water mixed, sugar, salt and pepper. Cover loosely and cook for 2 minutes on HIGH. Drain and serve

around the pigeons. Pour the sauce over the pigeons and the endive to serve.

## Pigeon Kebabs with Walnut Grape Pilaf

**PREPARATION TIME:** 20 minutes

**MICROWAVE COOKING TIME:**
14 minutes

**SERVES:** 4 people

3-4 pigeons, depending on size
8 strips of bacon/streaky bacon
30g/2 tbsps butter or margarine, melted

**WALNUT GRAPE PILAF**
180g/6oz/1½ cups brown rice
570ml/1 pint/2 cups stock and wine
    mixed
10ml/2 tsps thyme
120g/4oz/1 cup walnuts, chopped
1 small bunch purple or red grapes
Salt and pepper

Combine the rice with the stock and wine, salt, pepper and thyme in a large casserole. Cover loosely and cook for 10 minutes on HIGH. Cover completely and leave to stand 10 minutes for the rice to absorb the liquid. Add the chopped walnuts, cut the grapes in half and remove the seeds and add to the pilaf. Remove the breast meat from the pigeons and cut each breast half into 3 pieces. Thread onto skewers with the bacon. Brush each kebab with the melted butter or margarine and place on a roasting rack. Cook the kebabs 2 minutes per side. Set them aside, loosely covered, for 5 minutes before serving. Brush the kebabs with the cooking juices and serve on top of the pilaf.

## Quail with Apples and Calvados

**PREPARATION TIME:** 20 minutes

**MICROWAVE COOKING TIME:**
17-19 minutes

**SERVES:** 4 people

8 quail
2 large apples, peeled and thinly sliced
60g/4 tbsps/¼ cup butter or margarine

**SAUCE**
15ml/1 tbsp flour/plain flour
140ml/¼ pint/½ cup white wine or cider
280ml/½ pint/1 cup double/heavy
    cream
60ml/4 tbsps/¼ cup Calvados or brandy
30ml/2 tbsps chopped parsley
Salt and butter

Heat a browning dish for 5 minutes on HIGH. Melt the butter and brown the quail for 4-6 minutes, turning often to brown evenly. Remove the quail and set aside. Add the sliced apples to the browning dish and cook for 2 minutes, turning over often to brown on both sides. If the apples are not browning sprinkle lightly with sugar. Remove the apples and set them aside. Stir the flour into the juices in the dish and add the white wine and the Calvados. Return the quail to the dish or transfer to a casserole. Cover the dish tightly and cook for 5 minutes on HIGH. Remove the quail and keep warm. Add the cream and the parsley to the dish with salt and pepper. Cook for 1 minute on HIGH. Add the apples to the sauce and pour over the quail to serve.

## Pheasant Alsacienne

**PREPARATION TIME:** 20 minutes

**MICROWAVE COOKING TIME:**
28-30 minutes

**SERVES:** 4 people

2 pheasants, dressed
2 onion slices
2 sprigs thyme
30ml/2 tbsps oil

**ACCOMPANIMENT**
45g/3 tbsps butter
45g/3 tbsps flour
1 head white cabbage, shredded

**Facing page:** Pigeon Kebabs with Walnut Grape Pilaf (top) and Garlic Roast Pigeon (bottom).

2 apples, peeled and grated
30ml/2 tbsps caraway seeds
225g/8oz smoked sausage, sliced
280ml/½ pint/1 cup white wine
1 bay leaf
Salt and pepper

Prick the pheasants lightly all over the skin and brush with oil. Place the pheasants breast side down on a roasting rack, one at a time if necessary. Cook for 10 minutes on MEDIUM. Turn over and cook for a further 10 minutes on MEDIUM. Cook for 15 minutes on the Combination setting of a microwave convection oven, turning once. Cover and leave to stand while preparing the cabbage. Melt the butter in a large casserole for 30 seconds on HIGH. Add the flour and the wine and combine with the remaining ingredients. Cook for 8-10 minutes on HIGH, stirring frequently. Serve with the pheasants.

## Wild Duck with Limes and Onions

**PREPARATION TIME:** 20 minutes

**MICROWAVE COOKING TIME:** 25 minutes

**SERVES:** 4 people

2 wild ducks
2 slices onion
2 bay leaves
60g/2oz/¼ cup butter or margarine

**SAUCE**
45g/1½ oz/3 tbsps flour/plain flour
Cooking juices from the duck
280ml/½ pint/1 cup stock
2 onions, finely sliced
Grated rind and juice of 1 lime
Pinch of sugar
Salt and pepper

**GARNISH**
Lime wedges

Prick the skin of the duck all over and rub with half of the butter. Put an onion slice and a bay leaf inside each duck. Put onto a roasting rack breast side down and cook for 5 minutes on MEDIUM. Turn the

ducks over and cook for 10 minutes further on MEDIUM. Cook on the Combination setting of a microwave convection oven for 16 minutes. Turn over after 8 minutes. Cover loosely and leave to stand for 5 minutes. Combine the pan juices with the remaining butter in a small bowl, and cook 30 seconds on HIGH to melt. Add the sliced onions, cover the dish loosely, and cook for 2 minutes on HIGH. Stir in the flour, stock, lime juice and grated rind. Add a pinch sugar, salt and pepper and cook a further 5 minutes on HIGH, or until thickened. Pour over the ducks to serve and surround with lime wedges.

## Wild Duck with Blackcurrants and Port

**PREPARATION TIME:** 15 minutes

**MICROWAVE COOKING TIME:** 20-25 minutes

**SERVES:** 4 people

2 wild ducks
2 onion slices
2 sprigs thyme
30g/2 tbsps butter or margarine
450g/1lb can blackcurrants (if unavailable substitute other red berries or dark cherries)
15ml/1 tbsp red wine vinegar
140ml/¼ pint/½ cup port
15ml/1 tbsp cornstarch/cornflour
Pinch of salt and pepper

Prick the duck skin all over and rub each duck with the butter. Put a slice of onion and a sprig of thyme inside each duck and place them breast side down on a roasting rack. Cook on MEDIUM for 5 minutes. Turn over the ducks and cook a further 10 minutes on MEDIUM. Cook for 16 minutes on the Combination setting of a microwave convection oven. Turn halfway through the cooking time. Cover loosely and set aside for 5 minutes. Combine the blackcurrants with the port, vinegar, cornstarch/cornflour, pan juices from the duck, salt and pepper in a deep bowl. Cook, uncovered, for 5 minutes on HIGH or until thickened, stirring

frequently. Remove the onion and the thyme from the ducks and pour over the blackcurrant sauce to serve.

## Quail with Raspberries

**PREPARATION TIME:** 15 minutes

**MICROWAVE COOKING TIME:** 9-11 minutes

**SERVES:** 4 people

8 quail
225g/8oz frozen raspberries
280ml/½ pint/1 cup red wine
15ml/1 tbsp red wine vinegar or raspberry vinegar
15g/1 tbsp sugar
1 sprig rosemary
15g/1 tbsp cornflour/cornstarch

**GARNISH**
Whole raspberries and watercress

Prick the quail lightly all over with a fork and rub with a bit of butter. Put the quail breast side down on a roasting rack in a circle with the thicker part of the quail pointing to the outside of the dish. Cook for 2 minutes on HIGH. Turn the quail over and cook for a further 3 minutes on HIGH. Cook for 6 minutes on the Combination setting of a microwave convection oven without turning. Cover loosely and set aside while preparing the sauce. Reserve 16 raspberries for garnish and combine the raspberries with the remaining sauce ingredients in a deep bowl. Cook for 4-6 minutes on HIGH, stirring frequently to break up the raspberries. When thickened, purée in a food processor until smooth. Strain to remove the raspberry seeds. Cut the quail in half and coat with the raspberry sauce. Garnish with the reserved whole raspberries and watercress to serve.

## Dijon Rabbit with Capers

**PREPARATION TIME:** 15 minutes

**MICROWAVE COOKING TIME:** 34 minutes

**SERVES:** 4 people

*8 rabbit quarters*
*45g/3 tbsps butter or margarine*
*45g/3 tbsps flour/plain flour*
*280ml/½ pint/1 cup stock*
*140ml/¼ pint/½ cup white wine*
*140ml/¼ pint/½ cup double/heavy*
  *cream*
*30ml/2 tbsps Dijon mustard*
*30ml/2 tbsps capers*
*15ml/1 tbsp chopped chives*
*Salt and pepper*

Heat a browning dish for 5 minutes on HIGH. Melt the butter and brown the rabbit for 2 minutes on each side. Remove the rabbit and add the flour, stock, wine, salt, pepper and mustard. Return the rabbit to the dish or transfer to a casserole. Cook, covered, for 25 minutes on MEDIUM. Remove the rabbit from the dish and add the capers, chives and cream. Cook a further 2 minutes

on HIGH and pour over the rabbit to serve. Serve with French/green beans.

## Pepper Rabbit and Mushrooms

**PREPARATION TIME:** 15 minutes

**MICROWAVE COOKING TIME:**
34 minutes

**SERVES:** 4 people

*8 rabbit quarters*
*45g/3 tbsps butter or margarine*
*45g/3 tbsps flour/plain flour*
*2 shallots, finely chopped*
*280ml/½ pint/1 cup stock*
*140ml/¼ pint/½ cup white wine*
*225g/½ lb mushrooms, sliced*
*140ml/¼ pint/½ cup heavy/double*
  *cream*

**Left: Pepper Rabbit and Mushrooms (top) and Dijon Rabbit with Capers (bottom). Right: Wild Duck with Limes and Onions (top) and Wild Duck with Blackcurrants and Port (bottom).**

*5ml/1 tsp coarsely ground black pepper*
*15ml/1 tbsp chopped parsley*
*Salt*

Heat a browning dish for 5 minutes on HIGH. Melt the butter and brown the rabbit pieces and the shallots for 1 minute per side on HIGH. Add the stock, wine, pepper and salt. Cook, covered, for 25 minutes on MEDIUM. Add the mushrooms and cook a further 2 minutes on HIGH. Remove the rabbit from the casserole and stir in the cream and parsley. Pour the sauce over the rabbit to serve.

# INDEX